TOUGH LOVE

TOUGH LOVE

John Macey

OM
publishing

Scripture quotations are taken from the New International Version,
© 1973, 1978, 1984 by International Bible Society and published in
Britain by Hodder & Stoughton Ltd.

Briitish Library Cataloguing-in-Publication Data

A catalogue record for this book
is available from the British Library

ISBN 1–85078–114–1

OM Publishing is an imprint of Paternoster Publishing,
PO Box 300, Carlisle, Cumbria CA3 0QS, UK
http://www.paternoster.publishing.com

Printed in the UK by Cox & Wyman Ltd., Reading

Dedication

To my wife Anne, in appreciation of her patience and tolerance especially during the early years at the Centre.

1

Bells suddenly started ringing. The tranquil atmosphere of my intensive-care ward was transformed into a scene of frantic activity. Doctors and nurses materialised from nowhere, rushing to the unconscious form in the next bed. 'Thumps' came from behind the drawn curtains as electrical impulses sought to counteract a cardiac arrest. The monitor began to bleep: the doctors had succeeded in bringing another patient back from the verge of eternity.

Looking around I reflected how quickly my circumstances had changed. It was the last Saturday of October 1980 and only an hour earlier I had been at lunch with my wife Ann. The previous day I had arrived home from a strenuous week of teaching and preaching in Northern and Southern Ireland, and during my meal had complained of chest pains. I had agreed to drive over to Prince Charles Hospital, Merthyr, primarily to allay my wife's fears. After an ECG test, I listened in disbelief as the Registrar said, 'I think we'd better keep you in for observation.'

'But I feel fine now,' I protested. Ignoring my arguments she called the porters and said, 'Please take this patient to CCU Ward 10.'

'What on earth is CCU?' I asked the porters.

'Coronary Care Unit!' one replied, and we were soon speeding upwards in the lift. As I was wheeled into the small four-bedded ward, I was greeted by the Ward Sister, affectionately nicknamed Maid Marion, I later learned. Swinging my legs over the side of the trolley I was told in no uncertain terms by Maid Marion that under no circumstances must I exert any effort.

'Your feet won't touch the ground for the next seven days at least,' she prophesied.

As the porters lifted me into bed and the nurses connected me to my personal monitor, I began to wonder whether perhaps something serious had happened. At that point the bells had started ringing and doctors had run into my small ward with such urgency that I knew I was in the presence of life and death, time and eternity.

Little did I realise at that moment that the Lord had brought me into Prince Charles Hospital to show me needs and situations in my community that I would otherwise have been totally ignorant of. Now as I lay in the Coronary Care Unit, waited on hand and foot, there was plenty of time to reflect on recent events as well as to contemplate the future.

Just four months earlier, I had been inducted as a superintendent minister to pastor six churches in the Aberdare area at the head of the Cynon Valley in South Wales. Even though these were Pentecostal churches the majority reflected the spiritual condition of the valley. Small congregations consisted generally of middle-aged or elderly folk and it had quickly become apparent that none of them, even the largest church with a congregation of around eighty, had a vision or strategy for reaching their communities with the gospel; neither, I suspected, had they any idea of the needs and problems around them.

The small town of Aberdare, once a coal-mining community, had suffered badly from many pit closures. The valley population of around 80,000 was generally depressed and the social problems accompanying a very high rate of unemployment were breeding-grounds for many other ills. Empty chapels—a memorial to days of great spiritual activity—littered the valley. They were regarded only as proof that God was either dead or didn't care.

As a pastor I felt deeply challenged about how I, an Englishman and an outsider in this staunchly traditional Welsh stronghold, could make the changes necessary to communicate the gospel effectively, especially to the younger generation.

With these feelings my wife and I had gone on holiday to Bournemouth in September 1980. One afternoon we went into a local coffee shop and suddenly but quite definitely I heard the Lord speak to me, 'This is the way you are to do it.'

'Which way, Lord?' I asked. 'I don't understand.'

'Go home and open a Christian coffee shop,' the Lord said.

That was easier said than done in Aberdare. Not only was there the problem of finance but the even greater difficulty of breaking down restrictive traditions and motivating people to become involved in a ministry outside the four walls of their churches.

'It's a brilliant idea but I can't promise to support it. I can't see it ever happening—not in Aberdare,' one of my leading elders had said after I had taken him into my confidence about what the Lord had said to me. I was disappointed by this negative response from the man I had most expected to support me.

'But I've found the perfect place for it,' I responded, trying to arouse his enthusiasm. 'It's right in the middle of the town—a corner position with three floors and enormous potential. The only problem,' I added, as if by an afterthought, 'is that it's very dilapidated and will need renovating completely!' My excitement was obviously lost on my colleague, but as I left him I knew that what God had spoken to me in Bournemouth would happen. I was disappointed but not defeated.

The way to open the coffee shop had been shown to me in Northern Ireland just the week before my unexpected hospital stay, during a visit which ultimately changed the course of my life. I had conducted a weekend seminar in Belfast, and was due to move on to Dublin on Monday afternoon. As we were leaving the seminar centre on the Sunday evening, a young lady suddenly said to me, for no apparent reason, 'Did you know that Teen Challenge has opened a coffee house right opposite our church here in Belfast?' I didn't, but I was immediately interested!

I knew the Holy Spirit was speaking to me, linking Belfast with what he had said to me in Bournemouth and my vision for an outreach centre in Aberdare. I realised too that there was just time to visit the coffee house and see Roy Kerr, the Teen Challenge representative in Belfast, the next morning before moving on to Dublin the following afternoon.

Roy is a likeable man whose love for the Lord and for young people is obvious from the moment you meet him. He was the UK Field Director for Teen Challenge and had been responsible for inspiring and co-ordinating a thriving Teen Challenge work in Northern Ireland. Like most Christians who had been around in the sixties, I had heard the amazing story of David Wilkerson and his work amongst troubled young people in New York (told in his book *The Cross and the Switchblade*), but to be honest, that was about all I knew of Teen Challenge.

I found my interest growing by the minute as Roy said, 'What the Lord has done is fantastic—a real miracle! Teen Challenge is now working in over forty countries, reaching out on the streets and in schools and colleges to young people who need God's help. In fact, Teen Challenge is now the world's largest voluntary drug rehabilitation organisation. Our country desperately needs Teen Challenge; young people are dying on our streets because the church has failed to meet their needs.' It was hard to doubt his sincerity, and his enthusiasm was infectious. 'I've been praying for a contact in Wales, and I believe you're my man.'

Roy's mixture of forthrightness, love and Ulster

humour made him unforgettable. Before we parted, we had arranged for him to visit South Wales with a view to setting up a Teen Challenge work there.

I thought over all this as I lay in hospital. After three days I was discharged from the CCU ward and transferred to a general medical ward. My suspected heart attack was finally diagnosed as a hiatus hernia! To this day, however, I believe the Lord wanted me in hospital to open my eyes to human suffering, and to become aware of the desperate circumstances facing people daily in my parish. When it became known on the ward that I was a minister several people took the opportunity to share their problems with me.

Fred, a middle-aged man, was admitted about two o'clock one morning. He was very distressed and brought nothing with him. 'I've tried to take my life several times,' he told me later. 'I find life so unbearable that it often seems the only way out.' Fred's actions were obviously more of a cry for help than a serious attempt at suicide. 'My wife's addicted to bingo and spends every penny we have. When there's nothing left for food for the family she blames me and I can't take any more.'

'Why don't you ask your church for help?' I enquired.

'How can I? What would they understand? In any case, I don't feel good enough even to go inside a church.'

Anger seized me as I realised that here was a man with a genuine problem who thought the church was not interested in him. The next day he was due to be examined by a psychiatrist, but he knew that this would be no more helpful than it had been on other occasions.

We took it in turns to serve hot drinks last thing at night. One night a young woman I had not seen before brought my Horlicks and nervously enquired, 'You're a minister, aren't you? May I see you after I've done the drinks?'

'Why don't you speak to the chaplains? They visit you regularly,' I quizzed.

'They wouldn't understand if I did, and anyway I want to tell you.'

I listened with growing horror to the circumstances which had brought her into the hospital. She was a single parent with a baby of about a year old. 'Things were gradually getting on top of me and I couldn't cope. I was getting more and more depressed each day so I decided to take the baby with me to the top of the mountain at Mountain Ash and end our lives. Thankfully,' she continued, 'someone found us before we were dead.'

As I listened I tried to enter into her feelings of insecurity, inadequacy, frustration and ultimately suicidal depression. Outwardly she was an attractive young woman but inwardly she had suffered emotional crises and hurts far beyond her years. Now she was filled with guilt and remorse. I asked her the question I had asked Fred. 'Why didn't you go to a minister for help?'

'How could I?' she retorted. 'I don't know anyone in a church and besides I don't feel good enough to go to one.'

It was obvious that she did not consider that the church would have time for someone like her. I shared with her the simple facts of the gospel which she seemed hungry to hear. 'If you ask the Lord to forgive you and accept his salvation you will prove how much he loves you,' I assured her. We quietly prayed a prayer of commitment and I sensed that she had found the One who had promised always to be there.

As the days passed I felt increasingly that God was speaking to me clearly. More people were admitted suffering from overdoses and the effects of other suicide attempts and other patients opened up to me. I felt more and more certain that God had put me on my back to show me what appalling human suffering existed in the valley. Something had to be done. Generally, it wasn't that people didn't know about God, rather that they were totally indifferent to him or failed to understand his concern for them.

I realised that the Lord had drawn all the threads

together—the challenge I felt to evangelise those outside the church, the word from God to open a coffee house in Aberdare, his directing me to Teen Challenge, and finally his showing me in an unforgettable way the great needs in my own community. My consultant discharged me two weeks after I had been admitted. Within an hour I was home, and inside another hour I was in the estate agent's office asking, 'Is the property on the corner of Bute Street still for sale? If so, I want to buy it.'

God had rested, refreshed and challenged me. Now it was time for action!

2

Our manse lounge was full to overflowing at 8.00pm on the Sunday following my discharge from hospital. At the services that day I had invited anyone interested in a new evangelistic venture to meet at our home after church.

'Thank you for coming tonight,' I began, aware that soon I would be delivering what to many would be a radical package of proposals. 'I want to share with you what God has been saying to me over the past few weeks, and in particular during my time in Prince Charles Hospital.' I told the stories of people I had talked to, concluding, 'I'm convinced that the evangelical and Pentecostal churches in the valley aren't in touch with the people we're here to serve. There's a tremendous gulf between us—they won't come to our churches and by and large we're not going to them in a meaningful and effective way.'

Years of traditional thinking had cut deep grooves in the minds of some senior elders so that they found it difficult to accept new ideas and methods. For them evangelism was something done by the church and more often than not in the church. The idea of another organisation such as Teen Challenge being invited to help could well be too much for them to take. I knew it was important for me not to appear too critical of the past.

'I'm convinced that we must take the initiative and build bridges between our churches and local people. We must make ourselves available, take our wares into the market-place, so to speak. I believe the Lord wants us to open a Christian coffee house in the middle of town.' I stopped and listened to the silence! 'This has probably taken you by surprise but I'm sure it's the way forward. Equally, I'm sure that the new coffee house shouldn't be a denominational venture but should involve as many evangelical churches as possible.'

I sensed that this last statement had really 'put the cat amongst the pigeons'! Denominationalism was strong in the valley and there were probably no denominationalists stronger than my own. I told them of the way God had spoken to me in Belfast and of my meeting with Roy Kerr, explained a little about Teen Challenge, and ended, 'I'm proposing that we open a Teen Challenge coffee house.'

At that point some, including a few elders, 'switched off' but the younger members of my congregation responded positively. Someone asked, 'Will Teen Challenge provide the funds?'

'Teen Challenge, as I understand the set-up, is a faith ministry which seeks to share its vision for youth evangelism with local churches. It will provide training and if possible some voluntary workers as well, but the local group must believe God for all the necessary resources. We'll have to find our own finance.'

'How much will it cost?'

'That depends on whether we buy or rent the property. The estate agent has told me that rental will be £40 per week, but we can buy the building for £12,000. Whichever we do we must exercise faith and demonstrate it: we'll need to start a fund and invite people to sponsor the project.'

In 1980 property prices in the Cynon Valley were in a depressed state, and the asking price was very reasonable. However, the building I was after was in a totally run-down, almost derelict condition and thousands of pounds would need to be spent on it, regardless of whether we rented or bought it. The company which owned it was based in Birmingham and all negotiations had to be conducted through an appointed agent.

In my heart I knew it was the right place but it was certainly going to take a miracle to make it possible: the roof leaked badly, the first and second floors were sagging, ceilings were hanging down, the windows were rotten and it needed completely rewiring. New toilets, offices and a seminar room as well as the coffee house itself were all part of the plan and would add thousands of pounds to the cost of the project.

Humanly speaking it was a foolhardy venture, but the Holy Spirit had given me faith for the vision to become a reality. As I walked around the crumbling building I could see it finished in every detail and full of young people who needed Christ. All my inclinations were that we should try to buy the building but I could not get the agent to accept less than £10,000. I felt that £7,500 was the right figure and put my offer direct to the company in Birmingham. To the agent's amazement my offer was accepted.

'You must have someone on your side,' he laughed.

A year or so earlier one of God's 'saints' had made me a sincere offer which I now felt I should take up. 'I'm not a rich person,' she had confided, 'but if you ever feel God is telling you to do something and you need money, please come and see me. It's my ambition to die like John Wesley—penniless. All I have is the Master's; nothing belongs to me.' She meant it. I telephoned to arrange a meeting.

A few days later we were sitting in her lounge. 'I don't know what's brought you here, but I assume it has something to do with finance. How much do you need?'

She listened, obviously warming to everything I said, then exclaimed, 'Amazing, this is really amazing! After you'd phoned me I asked the Lord to tell me how much you needed. I felt the best way to help was to invest a capital sum and allow you to draw the interest. The Lord told me the figure was £7,500 but I haven't been able to invest it—I went to the building society to do so but it was closed.'

I don't know who was more excited—my friend, who felt so privileged that she had been chosen by the Lord to sponsor something he was about to do, or myself, as I realised that I had just witnessed my first financial miracle in the work of Teen Challenge. I drove home in wonder at the faithfulness of God, and in gratitude and humility that someone was prepared to give so selflessly, and that both he and she should trust me in this way. Another hurdle had been leapt over and I couldn't wait to tell everyone.

3

The telephone rang. To my surprise it was the managing director of the company in Birmingham.

'I thought I should get in touch with you concerning the property you've made us an offer on,' he explained, and my heart sank. 'We've had another, better offer,' he continued, 'and I must ask if you're prepared to match it. I have an offer in writing for £10,000 and I must make a decision this afternoon.'

'But,' I protested, 'you've already given me written confirmation of the acceptance of my offer of £7,500! Surely the honourable thing to do is to stand by your word.'

'I'm sorry,' the director said, 'but we're a public company and it's my responsibility to do as well for my shareholders as I can. However, I promise that if you match the second offer that will be the end of it—no dutch auctions.'

I was silent. What was I to do? I had been so sure that £7,500 was the right offer. Had I got it wrong? There was no time to consult all my newly-formed leadership team.

'What's your answer?' The voice a hundred miles away brought me back to reality and the moment of decision.

'All right, I'll take your word that £10,000 is final. I agree to pay it.' I put the phone down feeling confused but still certain that God was leading. In one of his daily readings on 'The Ways of God' Selwyn Hughes says, 'God reveals his will, then he reverses it, and finally he restores it.' I was at the reversal stage and my faith was being tested.

Not everyone in the leadership team agreed with my decision. One young man immediately resigned, along with his wife.

'You had no right to up the offer without consulting us. The Lord had confirmed the original figure and you should have stood by it,' he rebuked me. 'I can't be a part of the project any longer.'

I felt duly admonished, though more hurt by his outburst than anything else, and in a way I sympathised with him as I remembered what I was like at his age and reflected that I might have done the same.

'Why has the Lord allowed this to happen?' someone asked. Several people were shaken by this unexpected development.

'If only we knew the answers to that sort of question,' I replied, 'but often we don't, and then we must believe it's all in God's plan. Teen Challenge is a faith ministry and that's the secret of its power and success—a total relying on him for everything. The Lord asks us to move in faith and doesn't want us to become smug or complacent. If we can accept this as testing from the Lord he'll bring us through and meet our need.'

The next few months saw little happening apart from legal transactions making the property ours. The nights were dark and the days short and we had to wait until the spring before work could really begin. Meanwhile we threw ourselves into spiritual preparation for the task ahead, including the delegation of responsibilities for key roles.

I knew that if I did not do this I would be tempted to be involved in everything, and so it was a great relief when a team quickly formed itself under the leadership of Leighton Rees. Leighton and his wife Bev had a real heart for young people and their gift of hospitality meant they were never happier than when their home was like Piccadilly Circus with people milling everywhere!

During those winter months the Lord assured us of his presence and leadership and I was encouraged as funds began to materialise, often through the sacrificial giving of elderly members of my congregation. My 'saint' and personal intercessor continued to give as the Lord directed her, always on condition that her identity be kept secret.

Rebuilding work began in earnest in April 1981. Our leadership team was blessed with a carpenter, an electrician, a central-heating engineer who could also do general building and two or three of us who were just labourers. Since everyone was in full-time employment work could only be done on Friday nights and Saturdays.

We had set the opening date for the end of October, which gave us just six months, so clearly a miracle of another sort was needed. The initial rush of enthusiasm had died down and only the 'hard core' of workers was left, giving us at best a workforce of five men. However, we were proving daily that little is much when God is in it and I was certain we could meet our deadline.

Excitement grew as the shape of things to come gradually materialised. Townsfolk looked in and encouraged us, the local newspaper gave us good coverage, and despite many set-backs the work was getting done. The prospects of seeing *The Cross and the Switchblade* coming alive on the streets of Aberdare inspired and motivated us all.

The opening on Friday 30 October 1981 was exactly on schedule, despite our having to work around the clock the day before. Roy Kerr, who had so much to do with my own involvement with Teen Challenge, represented the UK board of directors and preached. We praised God for all that he had helped us to do since we first met almost exactly twelve months earlier. But the real work was about to begin.

The 'Oasis'—as the coffee house was named—was open Tuesday to Friday from 10.30am to 3.00pm and on Friday nights from 7.30pm onwards. I soon discovered a world of difference between preaching from the security of a pulpit and witnessing to Christ on the streets. Before long we had living proof that our town needed this new approach from Christians who cared enough to do something. Dozens of teenagers swarmed into the coffee house week after week, youngsters who had never attended church but were now challenged by the truth of a living Saviour.

Rose was our first convert. She was a young married woman who visited us regularly with her husband, Derrick, on Friday nights. They both attended the local Spiritualist church but Rose was far from happy with her spiritual condition and soon accepted Christ as her Saviour. Derrick was more difficult to convince and continued to attend the Spiritualist church, but Rose began to worship with us.

Shortly after Rose's conversion I realised how deeply we were upsetting Satan's authority in Aberdare. The Spiritualist church started Friday night prayer meetings to pray against the Oasis. Churches in the valley had been going about their business for years without disturbing the enemy but as soon as we started invading the streets with the gospel Satan got mad. My wife began getting obscene phone calls which became so bad we had to have all our calls intercepted. We were moving into a new dimension of spiritual warfare and things were beginning to hot up.

Two young American volunteers, Cheryl and Chris, arrived in April 1982. Cheryl came from Dallas, Texas, and Chris from a country town near the Canadian border. I worried—needlessly—about how they would adapt to valley life and to a culture so unlike their own—especially Cheryl, who was used to a very different pace of life in Dallas.

'Pastor John,' Cheryl assured me, 'if gaining local acceptance meant dressing up in a cat suit and standing on my head in the middle of the town I'd gladly do it!' 'I don't think that will be quite necessary,' I replied, 'but I do admire your missionary spirit!'

Their contribution to the Oasis quickly gave it another dimension. As full-time workers they were able to organise activities which had previously been impossible. School and college visits, street evangelism, prayer chains and nurture groups in their home for new converts all soon flourished. Young people started attending the local church in numbers not seen for years.

On a visit to a nearby college Cheryl and Chris met Paul, a local young man of 18 with a serious drug and alcohol problem. The girls returned to the coffee house and Cheryl excitedly announced, 'We've met a guy called Paul, and I know the Lord is going to save him. I suggest we put him at the top of our prayer list. He says he'd love to be a Jesus freak!'

Paul, a likeable fellow, was one of the town's 'in' crowd. While still at school he saved his dinner money to buy drugs, and when that could not satisfy his dependency he began dealing in amphetamines to finance his habit. Although he used drugs every day his weekends were times of heavy dosage so that he frequently spent the whole time without any real sleep. Drugs and alcohol usually ensured that Paul was 'out of this world' for the whole weekend.

Since he had been banned from nearly all the other pubs in the town, Paul's usual haunt was the Conway public house, just twenty-five yards from our coffee house. From there he visited the Oasis each Friday night during the summer of 1982—often with a pint of beer in his hand. Each week he would be witnessed to and would respond, 'I would love to be a Christian like you people. I really would love to kick drugs and drink, but I'm not ready yet.' Cheryl and Chris refused to give up and he remained the focus of much prayer.

Other contacts were made in the coffee house and on the streets. Rarely a Friday night went by without someone making a commitment to Christ. A fresh spirit of evangelism permeated the church as new converts brought friends and the church grew. Older folk were encouraged to continue praying and giving as they saw that their investment was not wasted.

'We've just had our first contact with bikers,' the girls announced as they returned from street witnessing one hot June afternoon. 'We saw two guys sitting on a wall outside a pub, so we told them Jesus loved them. One of them, Tim, got a bit up-tight and rode off. We'll see them again though,' they confidently predicted. 'Yes, another name for the prayer list,' said Chris enthusiastically.

Tim, a Hell's Angel, was in fact the son of one of our church members. He had been attracted to the 'Angels' at an early age and had thrown in his lot with them as soon as he could. Although still only 19 he was an obnoxious young man unconcerned about his personal appearance or hygiene. His waist-length hair was dirty and unkempt and his Hell's Angel outfit stank of a mixture of stale sweat and oil.

'He's going to be a difficult guy to get, but the Lord's going to save him,' Cheryl and Chris would often assure me. I wished I could share their faith! However, Tim did begin to visit the Oasis quite regularly but always at times when almost no one else was there. Although he would argue strongly against the fundamentals of the Christian faith he kept coming back.

He belonged to a Hell's Angel chapter based in Cardiff and was frequently involved in fights between rival gangs. Motor bikes, alcohol, drugs and violence seemed to be the main ingredients of his life and he became increasingly involved with the Hell's Angels despite weekly and sometimes daily counselling from Cheryl and Chris.

Then suddenly we did not see him for several days and learned from his mother that he had been involved in a serious motor-bike accident. Returning late one night from a Hell's Angel festival he had had a head-on collision with a van just outside Neath. He was somersaulted over the van whilst his pillion passenger ended up under it. Both men suffered serious injuries and were admitted to the intensive care ward at Neath General Hospital.

Cheryl was never one to miss a golden opportunity to witness—now that Tim was on his back it was just the moment to send him a book to read. When I visited him it was on his locker—*Hell's Angel*, Brian Greenaway's life story—and it had an immediate impact on him. 'If you can ever get a converted Hell's Angel to give his testimony at the Oasis on a Friday night, I promise I'll come,' Tim surprisingly told me. 'I'm not interested in listening to anyone else; he must be a converted Hell's Angel.'

This was a challenge I could not resist, but such people are not too easy to find. However, at about the same time I learned of an amazing conversion three years earlier at a campaign I had organised at Brynmawr, Gwent, when the speaker at the Saturday youth night had been Brian Greenaway. A local Hell's Angel had been converted that night. I invited him to speak at the Oasis in November 1982.

In August Tim was discharged from hospital but walked with a permanent limp and a stick. We all redoubled our prayers for his salvation.

During the summer months our relationship with Paul had continued to grow but he still refused to commit his life to Christ. His drug habit was as bad as ever and it was obvious that he needed an urgent miracle in his life if he was not soon to be in serious trouble. Often he would stagger home, reeling from the effects of drugs and drink.

Whilst walking home one night in this state he missed his footing on the pavement and fell into the path of an oncoming car. The driver screeched to a halt after narrowly missing the staggering young man and was horrified to discover that he had nearly killed his own son! At times it seemed the breakthrough with Paul would never come, but after five months of consistent witnessing it happened.

Cheryl and Chris were in Cornwall with Ann and me in September 1982, when the telephone rang one tea-time.

'It's Leighton here. You'll never guess what happened last night—Paul got saved! I'll tell you all about it when you get back.'

As soon as we arrived home a few days later we heard

the details. As usual Paul had been in the coffee house but instead of inviting him to the Sunday service, Leighton had given Paul his home address and assured him he was welcome to call whenever he wanted. The next Sunday evening Paul was sitting in the local park feeling depressed as he 'came down' from his drug weekend and suddenly pulled from his pocket the piece of paper with Leighton's address. He remembered the invitation and on impulse made his way to Leighton's home. It was there that the miracle happened.

'We talked for at least a couple of hours,' Leighton said, 'and then I challenged Paul to ask Christ into his life. Suddenly Paul said, "Yes let's do it!" and committed his life to Christ. Paul just sat there,' Leighton continued, 'and I went to make a cup of coffee. He shouted to me in the kitchen, "Leighton, I don't think anything's happening." I called back and told him to believe that the Lord had heard him and that he would soon feel God's power.'

'What happened next?' I wanted to know, intrigued.

'Well,' he began again, 'before I'd made the coffee a shout came from my living room, "Leighton, I think it's beginning to happen; I can feel something happening inside me!" Paul came running out to me, shouting and dancing and claiming that something powerful was happening inside which was making him feel clean and good. He couldn't sit down for at least an hour. It was obvious that something tremendous had happened to him. He's been in our house every day since and was in the prayer meeting last Tuesday.'

When I met Paul the transformation was unbelievable. He was bubbling over with the joy of the Lord and totally unashamed of sharing with anyone what Jesus had done for him. It wasn't long before he was baptised in the Holy Spirit and praising God in tongues. Because he was so well known in Aberdare the news of his conversion spread like wildfire and became the subject of many conversations in the public houses where bets were taken as to how long it would last.

The special evening had arrived, our converted Hell's Angel was ready to give his testimony, but Tim was nowhere to be seen! I felt cheated and let down. Tim was not going to get out of our agreement if I could help it. I ran to his home where his mother answered my loud knocking.

'Tim isn't here,' she said. 'I can only guess that he's down at the Conway.'

'Of course' I thought, kicking myself for not having thought of that myself.

Chris and I pushed open the door and looked inside the Conway. The fume-laden atmosphere was almost thick enough to cut. In the far corner we saw Tim, surrounded by about five of his friends. I walked over to him. 'Hello, Tim,' I said as he looked up from his drink. 'You said you'd be in the Oasis tonight to listen to your ex-colleague and I think you should keep your word. I'd like you to come back with me.' At this point a fellow sitting on the bar began laughing mockingly and dropping empty beer glasses. 'I've kept my part of our agreement, you ought to be man enough to keep yours.' Slowly Tim rose from the corner and pushed his way past his friends.

'Where are you going?' a girl asked.

'Up to the Oasis with these people,' Tim replied. We followed him out of the Conway into the clear, cold November night smiling to each other as we recognised the work the Holy Spirit was doing in Tim's life. Although we (and he) didn't know it, the count-down to his conversion had begun.

23 December 1982 will forever be an unforgettable day in my life. I had arranged to pick up Paul at 2.30pm from the Oasis to take him to meet my 'saint'. I was eager for her to see at first hand the way that God was honouring her faithfulness and sacrificial giving. On sounding my car horn outside the Oasis I was greeted by a very excited Paul.

'Tim's up in the prayer room and he wants to get saved.

He's prayed but nothing's happened. You'd better come quickly and do something!'

Tim and Paul had been close friends before Paul's conversion. Paul had at one time supplied Tim with drugs; Tim was the first person Paul witnessed to after his conversion and he had not stopped praying for him since. Tim looked up as I walked into the prayer room, which was as cold as it was outside.

'Hello Tim, what's happening?' I asked, trying to sound as relaxed and casual as I could.

'That's just it, Pastor,' Tim answered. 'Nothing's happening. I've prayed and asked the Lord into my life, but nothing's happened and I don't think the Lord wants me.'

Cheryl and Chris were in the room as well as Paul. It was easy to read Paul's thoughts from the expression on his face: would God let him down after all his witnessing and hard work on Tim?

I had never counselled a Hell's Angel before, but I was sure that he was no different from anyone else in God's eyes. I asked Tim if he was aware of anything—such as occult involvement—that could be a barrier between him and God. He said not.

So I suggested that I should pray and that Tim should then repeat a prayer after me. Thanking God for what he had already done in Tim's life, I asked for him to be given the gift of faith to receive Christ. Then Tim began to pray a simple prayer after me. We had scarcely said three sentences before Tim began weeping and shaking from head to foot. On his own he cried in a loud voice, 'I accept you, Jesus, as my Saviour!'

By this time we were all crying with Tim and joyfully praising God for the miracle taking place before our eyes. Tim joined in and tears of joy now flowed as freely as tears of repentance. He embraced me, clinging like a limpet. There was no doubt that a miracle had happened—it was clearly written on Tim's face. The sullen resentful rebellious look had gone, his face was shining and his eyes were bright. The cold prayer room too had changed as it had suddenly been invaded by the presence of the living Christ.

'Just wait until my mother sees me,' Tim laughed. 'She's not going to believe it. I must go home, have a bath and get rid of all my gear.' Here was the first evidence of the inward change. Tim had not bathed for six months; he wore nothing except his Hell's Angel leathers. I wished I could have been there when Tim met his mother, but it was right for him to go alone. She had prayed so hard and long for him that this needed to be her own special moment of rejoicing.

Our coffee house had been open for just over a year and already I had seen more miracles happen than in the whole of my previous ministry. The Lord had confirmed his word with financial and material miracles, with human miracles in the form of workers and with spiritual miracles as young people were saved and filled with the Holy Spirit. Tim's conversion could have been straight out of the pages of *The Cross and the Switchblade*, and was the final confirmation, if any was still needed, that Teen Challenge had a part to play on the streets of Aberdare just as much as in New York City.

4

As the work amongst troubled young people gathered momentum at the Oasis, we tried not to lose sight of our original vision to minister to people of all ages who needed help. As I had seen in hospital, there were many older folk who were hurting desperately and gradually we began to reach some of them, although more slowly and less dramatically.

One morning a lady in great distress rang our 'help-line', set up to offer a telephone contact with us for people in urgent need of someone to talk to, and advertised recently in an article about the Oasis in the local paper.

'I don't want to give my name, but I'm so depressed. I can't live without my tranquillisers and I feel so guilty. Unless I can get immediate help I'm going to commit suicide,' she sobbed at the other end of the phone.

She declined my offer to visit her, but we fixed an appointment at the Oasis that afternoon, and at the time arranged a lady in her mid-thirties appeared. Her name was Christine and she told me she'd found the 'help-line' number in the local paper. She was obviously in a very nervous state and had been for the past two years. I assured her that whatever her problem, God had the answer, offering her forgiveness and healing.

Slowly the story emerged: over a period of time she had stolen money from an employer who trusted her; he had been very good to her even when he found out, making her redundant so that she could pay him back out of her redundancy pay. But she was overwhelmed by guilt and shame, unable to put the past behind her and go on with life.

I explained to her the destructive power of sin and the way the devil exploits our weaknesses to destroy everything meaningful in our lives, taking away our sense of self-worth. I showed her that God could give her a new start, wiping the slate clean. She could be forgiven, born again.

Christine made a commitment to Christ there and then, and returned next day with her husband, who was unable to understand the change in her. After a few minutes' counselling he too became a Christian.

Besides Christine and her husband, an increasing number of people outside the youth scene discovered that the Oasis was a place where they could find friendship and a listening ear. My wife began a very effective weekly young wives get-together which resulted in some conversions.

But success always brings its own problems and the success of the Oasis was no exception. One problem we were facing was the need to provide after-care for lads, and sometimes girls, who wanted to become Christians but who found the pressures of the local drug scene too hard to handle. Paul and Tim had become effective witnesses amongst their old friends. This often resulted in their bringing lads with serious drug problems to the coffee house and to church.

Jeremy, a local drug addict, was always in trouble with the police. A tall, thin, pleasant young man with an Afro hair-style, his 'second home' was also the Conway public house. Like Paul, he would wander backwards and forwards between pub and coffee house. His constant smile was a mask hiding the many problems which were slowly destroying him.

After a time he began to attend our Sunday evening services. One night he responded when I asked those wanting to become Christians to come to the front. As I prayed for him I sensed a genuineness about his desire to receive the Lord but when he called into the Oasis the following week it was clear that he had not been able to maintain his commitment. He looked sheepish and a bit depressed.

'How can I kick drugs, man,' he asked me, 'when I'm living in a house full of other addicts? I went home from church determined to give God a chance in my life, but as soon as I went indoors I found my friends having a drug party. It's impossible to stay clean when your friends put so much pressure on you. They'll even give it to you when you don't want it. Man, I don't think I'll ever kick the habit.'

The need for longer-term help was becoming increasingly apparent; a place where such lads could be brought through the early traumas of kicking drugs and taught to live free through faith in Christ, a place where they could receive counselling and teaching and be filled with the Holy Spirit.

In one half-hour in December the Lord had delivered Tim completely. He had suffered no withdrawal problems and had also been able to quit smoking and drinking immediately. He had even received healing for his twisted knee so that he no longer needed to walk with a stick. But this would not always be the case: some addicts would need intensive help as well as a practical training programme to prepare them for future employment.

I sensed that God had led me into a work that would go far deeper than just the coffee house, and that soon we must set up a rehabilitation programme. The idea was stimulating and challenging, but all it would involve frightened me. Where would the money come from? What about staff? Where could we find a place? As always, the Lord had the answer to those and many similar questions.

Four or five months after his conversion Tim was restless. 'I feel the Lord is speaking to me about my future, but I don't have much to offer him. I've thought about going back to toolmaking, but I don't think that's what the Lord wants me to do. I think he wants me involved in Teen Challenge in some way.'

I have always been reluctant to recommend early 'full-time service' to young people because education and secular experience can be excellent preparation for future ministry. But Tim's conversion had been so dramatic and his stand for the Lord so strong that it was obvious God's hand was on him. It had taken great courage for him to face the leaders of his Hell's Angel gang and hand in the 'patches' which were the symbol of his membership—an act which demonstrated his determination to sever all links with the outfit.

But even that had not been sufficient to end it all and before he could consider himself truly free it was necessary to pay the gang several hundred pounds, a sort of buying-out procedure. These courageous acts were indicators of God's grace in his life and I was beginning to agree with him that God wanted to prepare him for a future ministry.

However, I reminded Tim how David Wilkerson learned to test his leadings—trying to ignore them to see if they would go away. If they did then he knew it was only his own mind but if they grew stronger, he knew God was speaking to him. I suggested that Tim adopt the same method. Tim agreed, but when a few weeks later he still felt the same I suggested that he should spend three months at the Teen Challenge Training Centre in Wiesbaden, West Germany.

'They run a three-month discipleship and training programme which will equip you to work with hurting young people,' I explained. This was a challenge to Tim's faith since to go to Wiesbaden would require considerable finance for his travel, accommodation and fees. Undaunted, he jumped at the chance, and booked himself into the first available course. When his financial needs began to be met we knew that this was the Lord's confirmation that Tim was doing the right thing.

It was now my turn to follow the good advice I had given to Tim, but I found that my conviction that Teen Challenge should have a rehabilitation centre just would not go away. In fact as the early months of 1983 passed my feelings on the matter grew stronger, to the point where I knew I had to do something. I shared my convictions at our next Teen Challenge board meeting and to my great pleasure I was authorised to make preliminary enquiries.

I knew that finding a place to begin would not be easy, especially in view of our nil resources. However, a building formerly used as a Bible School by the Apostolic Church seemed a possibility. It had been purpose-built in the late thirties to house a small theological college and it was able to offer accommodation for about twenty people. In many ways it was not ideal but at least it was a start! Its location at Penygroes, Dyfed meant that it was only thirty-five miles from Aberdare and it would be possible for me to travel to the new Centre at least twice weekly.

By the end of May 1983 arrangements had been finalised for Teen Challenge to use it. The Apostolic Church had generously agreed that we could use the accommodation rent-free for the rest of that year and begin a rental tenancy from 1 January 1984. Once again, the Lord was going before us and opening doors. At that time too the Lord was in the process of selecting our future staff team by dislodging people from their places of employment and preparing their hearts for some new, unknown ministry.

5

I had first met Teresa amongst the rubble of stones and building materials during early restoration work at the Oasis. An Aberdare-based social worker who had close working links with the probation service, her strong Christian commitment and obvious interest in helping people gave her a natural enthusiasm for our work and she became a great asset. Soon after hearing about the new development at Penygroes she asked to talk to me.

'During the past few months,' she began, 'I've become more and more disenchanted with what I'm doing. I've prayed hard about my future and I'm convinced that the Lord wants me to join the staff at the new rehabilitation centre.'

I could hardly believe my ears, and whilst I was delighted I also felt concerned for Teresa.

'Isn't that a rather drastic step?' Teresa was young and single, and job security was an important consideration. 'After all,' I continued, 'the rehabilitation centre will take some time to organise and we won't be able to pay staff. Everyone will have to trust God to meet their financial needs, so it's essential that you know you're doing the right thing.'

Teresa was undaunted. 'I guessed it would be on a faith basis and I'm fully prepared for that: after all, there's only me to think about. As for the organising—that's where I thought I could be most useful—by drawing on my experience in social services. I'd be happy to set up an office and do any public relations work necessary. I really want you to consider me and I'll be available from October!'

Our first staff members moved into the new Centre in July 1983. Julian and Heike, a young married couple with a lovely little son, had quickly responded to an invitation to join the initial staff team. Julian was a converted addict and since his conversion had gained experience working in a Teen Challenge coffee house in London. They were a young couple totally dedicated to serving the Lord and it soon became clear that they would not easily be put off by any hardships we might face in setting up our new work.

Things were progressing well. There were three new staff members including Teresa but we still needed another couple who would be 'mother and father' to the team and to our future referrals. Ideally they would be spiritually and emotionally mature, able to handle any situation from cooking to counselling, and from first aid to financial accounts. In short, we needed the very best but could offer them nothing except some rather substandard living accommodation. Where on earth would we find such a couple? I knew the answer to this question was the key to the success of the whole project and yet I realised there was nothing I could do to manufacture people with such qualities. It was up to the Lord to provide once more. Yet again it happened in a most unexpected way.

Our denomination's national Youth Camps were always times to remember because of the enthusiasm, openness and genuine fun with so many young people, but never more so than in 1983. Arriving at Kimnel Bay Christian Conference Centre, North Wales, I was greeted by one of the camp leaders who asked, 'Did you know that Ken and Betty are leaving Kimnel? They're due to go in about six weeks but at present have no idea where.'

Ken and Betty-Ruth Ogden were the warden-managers of the conference centre, having gone there some four years earlier when the magnificent old mansion needed major restoration. Ken, a qualified builder, had directed the renovations, and also done some of the more skilled work himself. That was all I knew of them, except that they were a very dedicated Christian couple. However, on hearing the news of their imminent departure from Kimnel I felt compelled to share with them the plans for our new project as soon as an opportunity arose. Within the hour I had bumped into Betty-Ruth as we were crossing the quadrangle. 'Hello Betty, nice to see you again,' I greeted her. 'It's good to be back at Kimnel, but is it right that you'll be leaving soon?'

'That's right,' she said. 'We're due to leave in about six weeks, but we don't know what the Lord wants us to do so we're waiting for his guidance.'

Before I knew what I was saying I had blurted out, 'I think I know just the right job for you!' As I said the words I realised how presumptuous I probably sounded, and hoped that Betty-Ruth would not be offended.

'Is that right?' she quizzed, adding with a rather reproving look, 'I'm always suspicious of people who know God's will for me. Let's have a chat later this week when we can sit down with Ken. I'm open to anything the Lord has to say.'

As it happened we got to know Ken long before that. At three o'clock the next morning his ability to handle a crisis was severely tested. My wife got out of bed feeling unwell, and to stop herself fainting grabbed the washbasin in our bedroom. Unfortunately it was not up to such treatment and came away from the wall with a terrific bang. As if that wasn't enough the cold water pipe fractured and began flooding the room!

Frantically I searched the corridors looking for the means to turn off the water supply, and although I must have found at least half a dozen stop-cocks, none of them made any difference to our room, which was beginning to look like an aquarium. I shall never forget the strange looks I got when I woke people at three in the morning with the words, 'Excuse me, but is there a stop-cock in this room?' Finally I decided there was nothing for it but to wake Ken.

'I'm terribly sorry this has happened,' he apologised, as if he had caused the problem. 'Let's get the water turned off.' I clambered with him behind secret panels and over newly-installed suspended ceilings and found the elusive device. Soon the mopping up had been done and Ken said, 'Let's pray.' His handling of the situation had been perfect and his ability to cope with the unexpected was proven beyond question. There was no doubt in my mind: Ken and Betty-Ruth were our couple.

'John,' Ken said as we sat in his living room later that week amongst half-packed boxes, 'I think we should explain how we came to be in this rather unusual situation. Earlier this year,' he went on in his soft Lancashire accent, 'we attended a Colin Urquhart retreat, and in one of the meetings the Lord spoke saying there were people there whom he was asking to change their employment. He promised that if they'd step out in faith he'd show them the next step. Both Betty and I felt the Lord was speaking to us so we came back and handed in our resignation.' Gesturing towards the boxes he continued, 'So here we are half-packed, ready to go anywhere the Lord leads us. One thing we do need, however, is accommodation.'

I felt myself warming to them as Ken spoke. Their genuine love for the Lord and total dedication to his will shone through in everything they said. 'What were you doing before you came to Kimnel?' I asked.

'Betty-Ruth is American; we met as missionaries in the Sudan, and spent twenty-five years in Africa. She was a nurse and I was a builder; we worked right through the Sudan civil war, Betty-Ruth on the medical side while I rebuilt churches that had been destroyed. We came back to the UK four years ago because it seemed unfair to our children to stay abroad any longer,' Ken explained. 'What we now feel is that the Lord wants us to be involved with young people. I'm sixty-two and want to devote the rest of my active life to helping build lives.' He then began to question me.

'What is it you feel we may be interested in doing? We'd love to hear about it.' By the time I had finished relating how the Lord had led us to open the Oasis and a rehabilitation centre I could see that they were hooked.

'It seems directly in line with what we feel we should do,' they both agreed, 'but before we make any final decisions we'd like to visit the new Centre and do some more talking.'

'Well?' I asked a few weeks later as they stayed with us in Aberdare. 'What do you think about it?' I knew it was a tremendous decision, especially at a time when most people are contemplating retirement, not a new ministry.

'Hmmm,' said Ken thoughtfully, 'the work certainly appeals to us and the prospect of living by faith doesn't frighten us—we've had to do that many times before and the Lord has always provided. What makes us just a bit hesitant is not being absolutely sure we have what it takes to do the job.'

'I want you to know that I'm sure you're the right couple for the job, but of course it's your decision,' I replied, trying to encourage them. I still had one ace up my sleeve, and now was the time to bring it into play. 'After dinner tonight I'll show you the Jesus Factor film about the Teen Challenge programme in the USA. It's the most challenging film I've ever seen and I'm sure you'll enjoy it,' I boldly declared. Sure enough, when we all retired to bed later that night I knew that God had clearly spoken to them about joining Teen Challenge. I sensed that our key couple had almost been recruited.

Tim returned from Wiesbaden in August 1983 full of enthusiasm. The further transformation in him was remarkable, both spiritually and physically. In Germany he had had his hair cut by stages, till on his return it was almost a 'short back and sides'.

'Pastor,' he said to me soon after he had settled into the coffee house again, 'I believe the Lord has some other work for me than the coffee house. I discussed it at Wiesbaden and Clive Beckenham feels I'm suited for rehabilitation work. I'd like to be considered for a staff position at the rehabilitation centre.'

I realised that although Tim was only 20 the Lord had done a remarkable work in his life. His wordly experience was certainly beyond his years and there was every indication that he would be able to exercise the authority necessary as a staff member. He didn't lack confidence either; in fact, the opposite was often the case. I was also pleased that Clive Beckenham was prepared to recommend him for full-time work in Teen Challenge. For some years Clive had been the Director of Teaching at Wiesbaden and I greatly respected his opinion and judgement.

'Well, Tim,' I replied, 'I certainly wouldn't disagree, but I think you should spend two or three months working here before we decide about your moving on to rehab work. You'll need to be prepared to trust the Lord for your support—there are no funds or resources to pay workers.'

By October, Tim was champing at the bit to move to the Centre. 'Please let me go down and help get the place ready,' he pleaded. 'I really believe it's where God wants me.'

'All right, Tim, but at first only on a trial basis. Let's see how you adjust to working with people in a team,' I advised.

Tim's arrival at the Centre brought our initial staff team up to six. Ken and Betty-Ruth had indeed joined the staff in October 1983, as had Teresa. With Julian and Heike, Tim made up the basis of a healthy unit. They trusted God for their daily needs and their total dependency on the Lord drew them together in a remarkable way as they proved that he was still able to supply all they needed. When money was short God sent food parcels—collections of food made in many churches—which became the main source of grocery provisions. Other essential needs were met by pooling their limited financial resources. The Lord was laying a firm foundation on which to build a strong future ministry. I wondered at the smoothness with which it was all happening—but storm clouds were gathering.

It soon became obvious that rumours were circulating in the village about our intentions, and since most were wildly exaggerated the need for explanations became pressing. Teen Challenge invited the villagers to a public meeting in the community centre on 27 October 1983, an invitation which was accepted by hundreds. It was a total disaster!

Since the meeting had been called by Teen Challenge the chairman insisted that it should open in prayer. This prompted an immediate and noisy withdrawal of about six villagers, loudly protesting that they should not be subjected to religious rites. As the meeting progressed (or, in reality, regressed) many feelings were expressed ranging from fear, prejudice and suspicion to open bitterness and hostility. The meeting ended with the majority making it clear that whilst they saw the need for someone to do something, they did not want it done 'in their back yard'.

The next few months would be crucial—increasing opposition would either destroy our morale or reinforce a determination to do what we all felt was God's will. Each day there was some new development—anonymous threatening phone calls, verbal threats of personal injury, petitions, marches and even a funeral wreath on the main gates. Notices were placed in windows telling staff that neither they nor Teen Challenge were welcome in the village, and our project was a constant source of interest for the local press as well as radio and TV.

During this troubled period great peace was experienced by the newly-formed staff team, despite all the turmoil. Promises from the Lord were a source of great strength to everyone and one, in particular, found its fulfilment the very day it was received.

One Sunday morning during their private meditations Ken and Betty-Ruth felt the Lord was giving them a promise—'Behold, I send you a deliverer out of Zion.'

'We don't know what it means,' Ken said as he shared it with the team, 'but we know God has spoken.'

That evening all the staff had been invited to take part in a service elsewhere, and on returning to the Centre it was obvious that something had been going on in our absence. There were large oil drums, stones and pieces of wood at the entrance to the car park though the whole place was deserted.

An explanation was soon forthcoming from a Canadian gentleman staying with relatives in the house adjoining the Centre. He had been appalled to discover the opposition we were receiving in the village. Then on his return from an evening chapel service he had discovered the entrance to our Centre barricaded and local opponents manning the barriers. Since the barriers were on a public highway he had asked that they be removed, but his request was refused despite his threatening to call the police, who on arrival duly instructed the culprits to dismantle the barrier.

By the time we arrived complete peace, and access, had been restored. We were amazed at the way the Lord had used a complete stranger to fight our battle for us, and even more so when we learned that he had returned from an evening service in a local chapel called 'Zion'. Truly the Lord had sent 'a deliverer out of Zion'!

The winter months of 1983 were spent drafting and re-drafting, revising and finally drawing up the Conditions of Residence and House Rules for our future students, to ensure that our programme would uphold the highest standards of Teen Challenge worldwide. Each student would spend about 11 months at the Centre, and it was vital to establish a spiritual programme which would not only communicate the life of Christ to our students but also discipline them in their new-found faith, and a structured programme which would develop self-discipline and yet retain a warm spiritual atmosphere to help them grow.

We were becoming part of the world's most successful drug rehabilitation organisation and it was vital that we worked with the Lord to produce the same results in our country. Some Teen Challenge rules might seem hard and difficult to enforce but we had to be guided by the years of experience the American programme had accumulated.

We had all done our homework thoroughly—visits to other Christian rehabilitation centres as well as a memorable trip to the Teen Challenge Farm at Rehrersberg, Pennsylvania, where an official investigation identified an 86% success rate amongst 'students' who had 'graduated' from the Farm programme. And since none of us had experience of working with drug problems we asked the American programme to send an experienced staff member to help us get established.

Bill and Debbie Dietrich arrived from Buffalo, USA in March 1984 and immediately added that missing something to our staff team. They threw themselves into the task of finalising the details of our future programme. Bill had been a student at Rehrersberg, and was looking forward to the challenge of applying all that he had learned.

We were grateful to the Lord for Bill and Debbie's arrival, but our feelings were not shared by everyone: signs began to appear in windows of village homes requesting, 'Bill and Debbie Dietrich go home. Americans are not welcome.' Once again the pressure of local opposition began to increase, and with it a growing sense of frustration that this pressure was keeping us from starting the rehabilitation programme after six months of preparation.

So I became convinced that the time had come for us to open the Centre to our first students—we could not wait any longer or be side-tracked from our purpose by local opposition. We decided to accept just two or three at first so that we could 'grow with the programme' ourselves.

The tension lifted once a decision had been made, and we were excited that at last things were going to happen.

It was quite a date to begin on—1 April 1984—April Fools' Day. By the end of twenty-four hours we felt that the joke was on us. Our first student was Derek, a married man with a drink problem who had finally decided to do something about it. His church supported his decision to come to the Centre and his pastor even accompanied him on the two hundred mile journey. The staff, elated at Derek's arrival, were devastated next morning when he decided he had made a wrong decision and wanted to go home!

'Lord!' we all gasped, 'what's happening? What are you trying to teach us?' We were left with Paul, from Aberdare. Paul had badly missed Tim when Tim left for Wiesbaden and Paul's inability to relate closely to other Christians made him very vulnerable. He showed signs of backsliding, and recognising his need of a discipling programme, came to the Centre in April. For nearly five months—till September 1984 when the programme really got going—Paul, and Chris who joined him from another rehabilitation programme, made up the student body.

So the Lord allowed us the luxury of starting with only two students. It was a time of learning for us all and 'starting small' provided an opportunity for the programme to grow slowly and quietly, thus proving to the local community that their fears were unfounded. All local hostility died down and we were able to establish and maintain good community relations.

April 1984 was a turning point too for Ann and myself. Inevitably the coffee house had begun to increase my work-load heavily. Cheryl and Chris had left Aberdare in March 1983, their year of voluntary service over. The gap left by their departure was enormous and very difficult to fill. I found myself more and more involved in visiting new converts, conducting nurture groups and running the coffee house as well as regularly working in six churches and pastoring the existing membership. It was an enormous load and was only possible by working a seven-day week.

Besides my local pastoral duties I was the National Youth Director for my denomination and served on several national committees as well. I had also been appointed to the UK Teen Challenge board of directors. These various responsibilities had increasingly begun to compete with each other for an even greater amount of my time and interest.

As a result, during the early months of that year, we had both felt increasingly that God was leading us into full-time work with Teen Challenge. But we knew the way ahead was not straightforward. Although we sincerely believed that God was calling us to take this step of faith, the last thing we wanted to do was to offend any of our spiritual leaders or congregations—yet we knew this might well be the case.

It was tremendously important to us that we should receive the blessing of our denomination's leaders and colleagues. We sincerely hoped that they would be able to give an honest endorsement of the way the Lord was leading us. It was one of the hardest decisions we have ever made, both having been brought up in the Apostolic Church, and after being in its full-time ministry for eight years, for almost all of which time I had been National Youth Director.

In May 1984 I was invited to present my case to the General Church Council, the governing body of the denomination. As I travelled to Bradford I was apprehensive about the outcome. Ann and I believed that the work the Lord was leading us into was as much a part of the work of the body of Christ as traditional pastoral care. One of our great disappointments was our denomination's apparent inability to embrace our vision and make it a part of the church's youth ministry.

I duly explained my position to the assembly and formally requested leave of absence from the full-time ministry of the church. To my delight, after due consideration, my colleagues laid hands on me to commission me. It meant that Ann and I would no longer be salaried or entitled to live in our church manse, but we knew the Lord would provide. Our service with the church would terminate in October 1984.

Our biggest problem was finding accommodation. We could not move into the Centre until Bill and Debbie moved out, and we could not afford to buy our own house. Rented property was unavailable and it seemed the Lord was testing our faith and commitment to the limit. Finally in desperation we arranged to put our furniture into store and at the end of October moved into a summer holiday chalet as a temporary measure.

The following weeks were the greatest trial of our faith; the weather turned bad and it rained incessantly for the whole of November. Each morning Ann and I awoke to find about half an inch of water covering the bedroom floor—the chalets were obviously not built to withstand Welsh winters.

It was much harder for Ann than for me—overnight she had lost her home, and had no idea when she would see her own furniture again, whereas the challenge of the whole project so motivated me that I honestly don't think I would have objected to sleeping in a tent. I realise now how insensitive I was to the problems our step of faith had created and in particular to the distress it caused Ann.

During those dark days we praised God for Ken and Betty's encouragement and inspiring example. Shortly before Christmas Bill and Debbie returned to the States and we were able to move into their small staff flat. We were still without our furniture but at least we were dry.

Apart from the Teen Challenge coffee house in Aberdare no aspect of my work had previously required me to act in faith as far as finances were concerned. Suddenly my relative security as a pastor with a guaranteed salary cheque every two weeks and a house to live in had disappeared, and unless the Lord provided our money there was none. Humanly speaking it seemed a very insecure situation, yet the excitement of having to trust God for our daily bread more than compensated for any loss of security.

I knew that if the rehabilitation centre was going to succeed it would need men and women of God who could 'make it happen'. Slowly our cash income increased as people gained a greater awareness of our work. Every Sunday evening we took services in different churches and this increased our support, both spiritually and financially.

The staff had all agreed that for the foreseeable future (in fact it turned out to be two years) we would receive only a personal pocket-money allowance so that the majority of any income received could be ploughed into establishing the work. In those early months we were thrilled as we saw the Lord meet our needs in many varied and unexpected ways.

The management at a Swansea chain store were sympathetic to our cause and donated to us all food past its shelf life. This meant that most Saturdays we would be invited to call at the store and load up our van. Since cash was in short supply this food was a real God-send, and what was even more exciting was the quality of the food.

In the words of Deuteronomy 8:7-10, the Lord had brought us into 'a good land...where bread will not be scarce and you will lack nothing', a 'land' of chickens (more than we could get even into borrowed freezers), yoghurt, cream, fresh fruit, cooked meats and usually other things many ordinary people could not afford to buy. Sometimes it was even best steak. We enjoyed all these good things, and praised God for his provision.

Now that Ann and I had moved into the Centre I was able to concentrate on establishing many essential features of the programme. Ken, a highly qualified builder, was responsible for the practical side whilst I looked after the teaching, counselling, administration and finance. It soon became obvious that unless we worked twenty-hour days we could never cope with the demands of such an intensive and highly structured programme.

In a wonderful way the Lord burdened other qualified men to help us on a part-time basis and soon Pastor Bill Lyons, Dr John Howell and Clive Evans joined us to help in the teaching programme. For Clive this meant a round journey of one hundred miles, twice a week, and for two years he and his wife Muriel faithfully honoured that commitment. These men not only ensured the effectiveness of the teaching programme—they also encouraged tremendously the rest of the staff as they voluntarily identified themselves with our ministry.

6

It was September 1984 and we were speeding west along
the M4, gospel music playing and the sun streaming in.
Andy was in the back reading and Peter sat silently beside
me. I couldn't help thinking how strange the situation
must seem to them. I recalled my first encounter with
Peter the previous month at our Oxford Induction Centre,
which we had opened earlier in the summer to give the
lads a place to spend the first month of their programme
getting off their drugs, alcohol and cigarettes. He epito-
mised the cliché 'once seen never forgotten'—loud, in
every sense of the word, overbearing and arrogant, but at
the same time his tremendous potential was obvious.

Bernard, who had come from Essex to run the Induction Centre with his wife Val, broke into my thoughts as
we sat around the lunch table. 'Peter's going to be an
evangelist one day—with a voice like his he won't need a
microphone!'

'That's right,' Peter chuckled, 'move over Billy Graham!'

A couple of weeks later both Peter and Andy were
ready to start the rehabilitation programme and I had
driven to Oxford to fetch them.

'I don't suppose that twelve months ago you ever
dreamed that you'd be in a car with a minister, listening to
gospel music and going to a Christian rehabilitation programme?' I laughingly remarked to Peter.

'Even two months ago I wouldn't have thought it possible—I can't keep up with what's happened to me since last July,' Peter admitted. For the next couple of hours he shared the events and circumstances which had culminated in his being on the road to Wales in search of a new beginning.

'My life was a mess even before I was born. My mother was only 14 so I was immediately put into care and for the next ten years I lived in children's homes. Although when I was about ten I was fostered out to good people I can still remember how lonely and vulnerable I felt, especially at school where I mixed with other children from normal homes.

'I took a lot of stick because I didn't have "proper" parents. I became very defensive and developed a sense of rejection and increasing bitterness as I got older. I was often bullied too, but when I was 13 I decided I'd had enough of being pushed around and started to get violent with people who tried to take advantage of me. At the same time I moved to a new school. It was an ideal time to live up to my new image. I carried out my first act of violence by plunging a chisel into a boy's arm.'

Peter continued his tale, describing to me how from then on his whole lifestyle changed as he gradually became more and more violent. Joining a local gang at 14 he began to enjoy fighting and hooliganism. Smoking and drinking had become regular habits with detrimental effects on his schooling so that he left at 16 with no qualifications. Employment was not too difficult since his adoptive father used some influence to get him a job as a labourer with British Leyland. Soon he found himself with more money than ever before and began spending most evenings in the pubs with weekends given over to football hooliganism.

His fighting usually took place on football terraces and even when the odds were against him he still tried to prove his reputation by fighting whole rival gangs alone. The violence would spill over onto the streets where pitched battles would take place until the police arrived. Inevitably he was eventually arrested—for fighting on the terraces during a particularly violent mass battle with Manchester United fans. But despite a £400 fine he found it impossible to stop fighting; he was addicted to fighting even more than to the alcohol which always released his violence.

'I enjoyed the respect my behaviour commanded from those I hung around with—it was what I'd always longed for and I didn't care that I was hurting and offending many people to get it.

'The football violence escalated as the need to establish ourselves as football's most feared supporters became even more important. Not long after my £400 fine, we completely wrecked the train in which we were travelling and went on the rampage through the town where it had stopped. Later at the match the police had to break up the battles and once again I was arrested and sentenced to six months in a detention centre.

'This was the Government's answer to the football hooligan problem—the short, sharp, shock treatment—but all it did was make me fitter—a better fighter when I was released. It certainly didn't cure my problem. The first Saturday after my release I was back on the terraces, but everything seemed to have got worse; the violence had become even more vicious and I needed to re-establish my reputation as the wildest and craziest fighter of them all. I was full of bitterness, hatred and jealousy as a result of my lack of identity and I felt completely justified in my behaviour.'

The fighting spread to many grounds around the country. At Liverpool, Everton and West Bromwich Albion bricks, chains, baseball bats and bottles were used as weapons and they regularly left 'enemy' supporters unconscious and severely beaten up. Evicted from his digs by the landlord, Peter broke into his house, smashed it to pieces with an iron bar then waited for him to come home. Fortunately, the police arrived first and Peter was sent to

Brockhill Remand Centre. He was sentenced to two years probation on condition that he lived at a Probation Hostel at Bilston, Wolverhampton.

'I went to the Probation Hostel realising that unless I could change I was destined for a life of crime and destitution. I hoped new surroundings and different people would be the answer, but it wasn't long before I realised that my alcohol and violence addictions were more deeply ingrained than I'd ever imagined. Soon I became a member of the Subway Gang which was committed to organised football violence. It was the same pattern all over again, only this time even more sinister and evil.

'We concentrated on away matches, and ran away from fights laughing, on a high which the excitement and violence had given us. We honestly felt that we were immortal; we could handle anything and live forever. By this time I had been given the nick-name "Animal" because of my outrageous behaviour and I was intoxicated by my violent lifestyle. Opposition supporters were like a red rag to a bull. Miraculously I managed to escape serious injury, but I knew I was dicing with death and that sooner or later I would be badly hurt. One New Year's night my stomach was slashed open and I was rushed into Wolverhampton Infirmary for an emergency operation.'

In hospital he heard about Jesus for the first time, from the lad in the next bed. Peter didn't want to know. He was in the unbreakable grip of aggression, anger and an insatiable desire for revenge. And so it continued, a life of uncontrolled aggression and destruction. He was also very bigoted and arrogant. His extreme racial prejudices often led him into violent exchanges, especially with Pakistanis. He had joined the British Movement and the skills learned on football terraces were now employed in pub brawls with black people. His racial hatred eventually put him behind bars again for six months for criminal damage, racial abuse and causing an affray.

Even this prison sentence did not change his attitudes or intentions. On his release he moved back to Birmingham, wandering from one shelter to another until eventually he took refuge at night in public toilets and subways. Football violence still dominated his lifestyle, which was by now offensive even to his friends. In his increasing isolation, drink became an even greater problem.

'About this time I made contact with some Christians from the Methodist Central Hall in Birmingham. Despite my aggressive behaviour, my skinhead appearance and abusive language they never gave up on me. Even when I physically abused them they still insisted that Jesus loved me, and in some ways this only made me even more mad. On one occasion I took a knife to one young Christian and screamed "Go on! Just witness to me and see how long you last."

'My way of life became crazier and crazier and I knew I couldn't handle it. Desperate to prove I was still number one, I stepped up my involvement in brutality and destruction. One Saturday last June I joined a local gang of "queer" bashers and for about twenty minutes outside the Albany Hotel in Birmingham we kicked and physically assaulted a group of homosexuals we'd cornered. I remember laughing as I cracked a bottle over the head of one of my victims, to the horror of a group of American tourists staying at one of the most exclusive hotels in Birmingham. As we ran away we spotted a group of Pakistanis and once again the carnage began. Then we made for a local pub to celebrate our victory.

'Later that evening walking past a local nightclub we spotted another group of Asians. This was our third rumble in almost as many hours. Whilst this fight was at its height the police arrived and dragged me away screaming abuse at our innocent victims. I was thrown into a police car and transferred to a cell where I had time to reflect. I fully expected to be charged with several serious offences which could lead to a long term of imprisonment so you could have knocked me down with a feather when after only half-an-hour a police officer announced, "Get up, we're letting you go." I could hardly believe my luck!

'Looking back I can see the hand of God on my life even during those wild days: following my unexpected release, my friends from the Methodist Central Hall suddenly increased their attentions. Although I did nothing to show that I was interested in what they had to say I could not help secretly acknowledging that they were different from everyone else I'd met.

'Their pressure increased when the Billy Graham Crusade began at Aston Villa football ground, and on 31 July this year they finally succeeded in their valiant efforts to get me to go. Not that I was really interested in Billy Graham but they'd promised me a free meal afterwards. Well, as you know I went and, hey-presto, the Lord did what everyone else had been trying to do for years. He got through to me and told me the facts about myself in a way I couldn't deny. For the first time in many years I heard the truth.

'When I responded to Billy Graham's appeal I knew something dynamic had happened but it soon became clear that years of bad habits and attitudes wouldn't disappear overnight. If I was to grow as a Christian I needed to get out of Birmingham, which was full of bad memories as well as too many temptations. I remember saying to my Christian friends, "You must get me out of Birmingham in the next week. If God really wants me he must work a miracle for me." By the end of the week I was in Teen Challenge at Oxford. God did it—and so, here I am!'

Looking at Peter I knew that God had done something very special. My own ministry was moving in a new direction and although I felt somewhat apprehensive I could not help feeling excited. Even the grey, austere walls of our Centre seemed inviting as we drove into the car park. 'Gentlemen, this is your new home. We've arrived.' They climbed out of the car, little realising what lay ahead. Neither, in many ways, did I!

7

'Hello, it's Jim here,' said a rather husky voice at the other end of the phone. 'I'm due to come to Teen Challenge. I've been in hiding for the past few weeks so it was impossible, but I think it's safe to come now, if that's OK with you.'

I assured him we were looking forward to his coming and a few days later Jim arrived. He was our first black student and he brought a new dimension into the programme. It would be interesting to watch the interaction between Peter and Jim since both were outspoken with fixed opinions—Peter's association with the British Movement had created very firmly held views about black people. Now would come the acid test—how deeply and effectively had Christ's love done its work in their hearts?

It rapidly became obvious that Jim, or Big Jim as he was soon affectionately known, was an excellent mixer, and despite his expert use of sarcasm he won acceptance from staff and fellow students alike. A six-foot tall, gangling young man, he bore the scars of a physical, emotional and spiritual rough time. I was Jim's counsellor, and soon the details of his unhappy past emerged.

'I was brought up in Liverpool,' he started, 'and put into a foster home at five. My foster parents were good to me, but I could never adjust to an all-white school and as a young lad went through my own hell. I knew I didn't belong to anyone and the loneliness and rejection I felt made me do unacceptable things—I'd lock myself in broom cupboards and force the teachers to break the door down. Later I found myself smashing up classrooms—my frustration drove me to such anti-social behaviour that eventually I was referred on to a school for maladjusted children. Sometimes,' he laughed, 'I think it was really a maladjusted school; it did nothing to change or help me.'

As I listened I realised that Jim, like so many others I was now meeting, was born with a less than even chance of ever making something of his life, the victim of circumstances over which he had no control but which, humanly speaking, had dealt him a very bad hand.

'At 16,' Jim continued, 'I decided I'd had enough of being told what to do and I ran away to the bright lights of London. I don't know what I expected, but there certainly wasn't a reception committee waiting to meet me,' he quipped. 'I looked pretty grown-up but inside was a frightened little boy and I didn't at all enjoy sleeping on a seat at a main railway station. The next day I walked around some of the famous places in London, and especially remember Piccadilly Circus. I was horrified by the sight of junkies lying around in the subway, some with needles still in their arms, and I swore I'd never end up in such a mess. Bit of a joke that, wasn't it?' he said, with a wry smile.

'But what could I do?' Jim asked. The question was clearly rhetorical. 'I was just 16 and penniless, an obvious target for exploitation. I soon learned that no one owes you a living and you have to get by the best you can, often by taking what you want. I joined gangs of other youths and got involved in all sorts of illegal activities.

'Soon I met a girl who had her own emotional problems and whilst we fell in love with each other it was probably our hurts that drew us together as much as anything else. We decided to live together and found a flat in the East End of London, where I continued my illegal activities. It seemed a pretty good arrangement for us both; we had each found somebody with whom we could have a meaningful relationship. But this didn't mean that I was pre-

55

pared to live a "normal" life, and as long as Jane got enough money she didn't care too much where it came from.

'I could cope with this way of living even though I knew it was wrong. We had our own code of morality—we called it the Bethnal Green Code—which included no burglaries and no mugging old ladies. Basically it was OK to rip off the rich and people who could claim it back on the insurance. Shop-lifting on a grand scale was my main occupation. It was quite possible on the right day of the week to score £1,000 or more on one expedition.'

'But,' I asked, 'if you were able to get by, albeit on illegal activities, when did your life fall apart? What happened to get you into the desperate condition you ended up in?'

'I got involved with the drug gangs,' said Jim with a touch of regret. 'The money was so good I was tempted to become part of an East End drug set-up—supplying to junkies. Some bread-heads moved into the area and I started working for them.'

'Bread-heads?' I asked, 'What on earth are they?'

'Bread-heads are in the drug game simply for the money; they never take the stuff and so get rich on the backs of junkies. The trouble was I couldn't keep from using the junk and I became a smack-head. Because I was pushing, it was easy to get my supply at first, until I ran up debts of thousands of pounds with my supplier, and then I was in real trouble.'

'How did all this affect your domestic life?' I enquired.

'It almost destroyed my family. By this time we had two young boys aged four and six, and although Jane refused to marry me we were faithful to each other and we really wanted to keep the family together. I can't blame her for not wanting to marry me—at least she had her own Social Security book which guaranteed her financial independence. She knew if I got my hands on that she'd never see any of the money. She became ill as the pressure of living with an addict began to tell on her, but that only made me turn to drugs even more. Jane's depression could only be controlled by medication. Imagine—I was stoned out of my head most of the time and Jane was doped up to the eyeballs on prescribed drugs, and in the middle of it we had two little boys who badly needed our love and protection. What a mess we were in—it's almost unbelievable!' Jim recounted.

'Unbelievable' was the word, I thought. Jim was our first heroin addict and he was introducing us to the real world of addiction—a world of misery, suffering, pain and disaster from which no one was immune.

'You see,' Jim continued, 'because of our problems, the boys were in constant danger of being taken into care—something I dreaded because of what I'd been through as a kid. Yet even this couldn't stop my habit and gradually things got worse. My drug debts escalated and this led to frequent violent attacks on my home. My supplier would send the heavy gang to get at me—my life-expectation at that time wasn't too good. We lived on the first floor of a block of flats and as protection I bought a Dobermann dog—more than once she fought off my attackers, but it was always a losing battle—I knew they'd be back. You can't take on an organised drug racket and win, and I knew that unless I paid my debts I'd end up seriously hurt or even dead.

'Of course, people owed me a lot of money for the drugs I supplied and I had no option but to lean on them pretty heavily. The drug world's vicious—dog eat dog—and you just can't afford to let anyone rip you off. When someone smashed my door and beat me up I'd go and find customers who owed me money and do the same to them. If they couldn't pay it meant a broken arm or leg; that's the way it had to be.'

'But how could you injure someone just like that? It's a pretty horrible thing to do,' I rather naively asked.

'Pastor man,' Big Jim replied, 'when your life and family are under attack you don't stop to think or even care. I just let my mind be filled with the hatred and bitterness boiling inside me and then it was easy to bring an iron bar down on a junkie's arm or leg. Anyway, it's the only way they'd respect me, although I realised that I couldn't go on running forever; it was getting harder every day. But though I often longed for a way out I felt trapped because there wasn't one.

'I knew I was destroying the people I loved. I remember seeing the look on Jane's face when I stumbled into the flat, shot-up in the bathroom and then lay stoned on my bed for the next day. It was no life for her or the kids. In the end she couldn't take any more and had a mental breakdown. She was admitted to a hospital in Mile End. Whilst in hospital she had a definite spiritual experience—she thought she'd seen the Lord—and after she came out she started going to a new charismatic fellowship in Whitechapel Road. The folks there showed quite a lot of interest in her and the kids, but although she wanted me to go I never did. As long as Jane was off my hands I was free to get stoned, so it was quite a good arrangement.'

Jim paused and shook his head, his broad grin lighting up his whole face. 'I suppose I should have known he'd get me in the end. I remember the first time anyone ever witnessed to me—it was almost too unbelievable for words. I was lying on my bed completely stoned as usual, when I heard a knock at our front door. I staggered to open it and found a rather small, very middle-class young woman there.

"Good evening," she began, "I'd like to introduce you to my friend."

'I blinked', said Jim 'and then I rubbed my eyes and looked up and down the alleyway. "Lady," I said, "whoever it is that came with you, I think he's done a runner because there's no one with you now!"

"Oh no," she replied, "you don't understand. I want you to meet my friend the Lord Jesus Christ who is always with me."

'Pastor,' Jim said, 'I have great respect for what she did but man, she wasn't real. There she was, middle-class, well-spoken, but totally out of touch with an addict like myself. Needless to say, I told her in no uncertain terms what she should do—and her friend. But she didn't give up, because other people from the fellowship started visiting me, much to my annoyance at first.

'How do you mean "at first"?' I quizzed. His story was intriguing and I found myself hanging on every word.

'Well, about that time the heavy gang began leaning on me much harder, and to keep them at bay I offered to pay my debts at £30 per week, although I knew it was extremely unlikely I could do so. At least it bought me a little time before things got really rough. Jane had told some of her friends at the fellowship, with the result that a young guy, a student, came to see me one night.

"Jim, I know the problem you're in, and I've come to give you £30. I believe the Lord's told me to give it to you," he said.

'I laughed at him. "How do you know I won't go straight out and buy more drugs, clever guy?" I asked.

"Because the Lord knows what you'll do with it, and he wouldn't have told me to give it to you if that's what you would do," this student confidently replied.

'What impression did that make on you?' I asked. 'What did you do?'

'I took his money, even though I told him I didn't believe all the God stuff. Strangely enough, though, I didn't spend it on drugs but used it to pay my debt that week. But I owed thousands and I knew I was on a loser. It was then that the same student offered me refuge in his flat, on condition that I would stop using. Because so many people were after me I had no option but to go into hiding—cold turkey and all. After two days in this secret accommodation I was in the hell of withdrawal. My friend absolutely refused to allow me to get any drugs and I began throwing up all over his living-room carpet. I can remember it now; I thought I was dying as I rolled around the floor, and then I could hardly believe what he was suggesting. "Why don't you ask the Lord to save you?

59

He's ready to help you as soon as you call on him," he said.

"Religion was no part of the deal, so get off my back," I snapped.

"What have you got to lose except your pain?" he replied. When he put it like that, I decided to give God a chance. "Lord," I cried, "please help me; please get me out of this mess." To my amazement something marvellous happened. The pain eased, my withdrawal symptoms subsided and I knew God had heard me. I could hardly believe it but there was no denying it—a miracle had happened. God had touched me! After that the fellowship decided to try and get me into Teen Challenge, and here I am to prove it. I don't think it's going to be easy but I know it's my only chance.'

8

I was rapidly discovering that truth is stranger than fiction. No one could possibly have imagined the complex lives of the young men who now began arriving at the Centre in increasing numbers.

Peter and Andy were beginning to settle into the new lifestyle of the programme but Andy was experiencing severe emotional problems. Two days after their arrival I was summoned to the bathroom area by a loud shout from Peter. 'Quick Pastor—Andy's done himself some mischief.' I raced to the bathroom to find Andy, razor blade in hand, standing over a wash-basin, silent and dazed as blood flowed from lateral gashes on his arm.

'Andy, whatever have you done?' I asked, putting his damaged arm under the cold water tap. 'Peter, please find Sister Betty as quickly as you can.' I put my arm around Andy to try and comfort him. 'I'm sorry,' he kept repeating, 'I'm sorry—it's the pain that made me do it. Not the physical pain but the emotional pain, the pain of the past, my memories, my hurts; sometimes they get so great that I feel I'm going mad. Slashing my arms is a way to suppress it all, the physical pain blots out the rest.'

'Come here, my love; let's have a look at you.' Sister Betty was on the scene and in her usual firm but understanding way had the situation under control. The arm was soon bandaged, but the next day Andy did exactly the same again. It dawned on me that this was his way of testing our acceptance of him—would his behaviour alienate him from us as it had done from so many people in the past? Was our love conditional?

'Andy, I want you to know that I and all the staff here really love you. None of us is perfect, but through the love of Christ we're able to accept each other just as we are. You don't need to do these things to test us, we're not going to throw you out or reject you,' I assured him.

His face brightened immediately. 'That's my problem; that's just it. I find it so hard to trust people or even to accept anything good they do for me—I always suspect their motives and then try to offend them so that I can justify my feelings of rejection. Thanks for letting me know it's different here.' He never slashed his arms again.

I was quickly learning much about the Lord's dealings with these troubled young men. As the programme's disciplines began to bite into their personal lives the Lord brought to the surface many things which needed his healing and delivering touch. I soon realised that these lads were not like ordinary members of an average congregation—in many ways they were more honest about their true feelings and refused to pretend things were OK when they weren't.

Soon Peter's basic problems with authority surfaced: every day he seemed to have a run-in with Bill. This often resulted in lengthy counselling sessions during which the Lord would unpeel yet another layer of his onion-like past. I knew it was painful for Peter and others experiencing similar things, but the breaking and stripping process was essential if the Lord was going to rebuild the real man.

'I feel so bitter and angry,' Peter would often say. 'I just can't let the Lord deal with me because I keep remembering people who have hurt me or ripped me off. You say I must learn to love them, but to be honest, it's doing my head in.'

'That's exactly what you must do,' Bill told Peter. 'You

must consciously forgive everyone who's ever wronged you. Go away and make a list of their names; then pray for God's love so that you can forgive them. Work through the list one by one until you feel God's peace replace your hatred.'

Peter did as Bill suggested and for the next few weeks prayed through his list of some 125 names. It was a challenging task, especially since number one was his mother whom he had never seen, but he gradually prayed through to victory. The rebuilding process had begun.

Others experienced similar victories. One morning at coffee-break there was a knock on my office door and Big Jim walked in. He looked rather sheepish as he stood towering over me and then suddenly thrust his hand into his trouser pocket. 'Here,' he said, 'take these. I can't stand it any longer.' He threw some cigarettes and matches onto my desk. 'The Lord's been convicting me about smoking and especially the deceit of trying to do it without getting caught. I honestly believe the Lord wants me to conquer it, but even if he didn't I can't stand the hassle of trying to get away with it,' he confessed laughingly.

I rejoiced at the growth taking place in Jim's life, but I knew there were other problems threatening to destroy his new faith, not least the situation back in London with Jane and the children. He often came off the phone looking depressed and although he did his best to put on a brave face I realised that things at home were not good. One morning it all came to a head as he stormed into my office after prayers.

'I've been here six weeks now and I've suddenly realised it's not the place for me. I don't like it, I don't belong and I'm going back where I can cope—the streets of London. I should never have let them talk me into coming here in the first place.' He stormed out again and ran to his bedroom, with me in close pursuit. Clearly he did not mean what he was saying and his frustration showed through the tears in his eyes. I watched as he began throwing his clothes into a bag. 'Jim,' I said, 'you know you don't mean what you're saying. You need the Lord; you need this programme; don't throw it all away.'

'I don't belong here,' he shouted back at me. 'It's not my scene. I belong on the streets. I feel at home there; I'm going back to the needle.'

Although I had never before been in such a situation I knew it was impossible to talk constructively because of the highly-charged emotional atmosphere. I tried another approach. 'Well, before you go Jim, let's have a talk. Then if you still want to quit, I'll take you to Swansea.' To my relief he accepted the suggestion and followed me back to my office. Once there he started again.

'You don't know how painful this place is,' he protested. 'I feel as if I'm naked; everything's been taken away from me; even the clothes I'm wearing don't belong to me. You tell me it's wrong to hate, but I need to; it's my driving force. You tell me it's wrong to live with a girl unless I'm married; you tell me it's wrong to steal but that's how I survived for years. Man, I feel scared of this place, I don't like it and I don't like what you teach.' He stood defiantly, waiting for my response.

I didn't know what to say, but the words came: 'Jim, this is not my place or my programme or my teaching. It's the Lord's place and he brought you here because he loves you. You may not like what you're being taught, but I'm prepared to offer you a challenge.' Jim eyed me, wondering what I was about to say. 'See this,'—I held up my Bible—'It's God's Word, his blue-print for our lives. It's also our textbook in Teen Challenge as well as our final court of appeal. If you're prepared to go upstairs for an hour and read it and then show me one thing in it that contradicts anything you're being taught in this programme, I'll resign as Director here and now.'

'But,' I went on quickly without giving him time to answer, 'if you find that all we're teaching you is the Word of God, I want you to give in to God. Is that a deal?' I waited for his reply. There was silence and then a large grin broke over Jim's face. 'You've got me there, Pastor. I already give in.' The round was won, but not yet the fight. It was inevitable, given Jane's situation, that there would be more storm clouds looming. They broke very soon.

'It's happened, Pastor,' Jim groaned. 'My kids have been taken into care. Jane's been hiding it from me so that I wouldn't leave, but tonight she blurted it all out; she just can't cope. The kids weren't going to school and the social worker's had them put into care. Ironic, isn't it? Now I don't want to leave I've got to—I must get them home as quickly as possible. I feel really let down by the fellowship. They promised to look after Jane but she hasn't seen them for weeks. Can I phone my housegroup before I leave in the morning?'

My heart was heavy for Jim and his family but I knew there was little anybody could do to stop Jim doing what he knew he must. However, I was determined to arrange for him to re-enter the programme as soon as possible. 'Use my office phone to speak to your housegroup leader, Jim. You'll find it a bit more private. I think I'd better stay, though.'

Jim's disappointment and sense of being let down was impossible to hide as he spoke to his housegroup leader. 'You gave me your word that you Christians would look after my Jane and the kids. Each time I've spoken to you I've been told that everything's all right, nothing to worry about. As far as I'm concerned you've conned me, deceived me and let me down. The things you sent me here to sort out—lies, conning, deceit—you need to sort out too. If that's Christianity I don't want to know.' He slammed down the phone. 'Well, that's that then, I'll have to go in the morning.'

'OK,' I replied, 'but if I can arrange for you to return, would you come back?'

'How do you mean? It's impossible,' he said despairingly.

'I mean, if we could get Jane and the kids out of London where they could be looked after?'

'I think she'd jump at the opportunity, but where? And who on earth would do that? And hey, don't forget my dog, she's part of the family as well, you know!'

Getting Jim's family out of London was certainly a big challenge, but long term it was the only answer anyway. His contacts and enemies in the East End made it unsafe for him and it was not the environment for his children to grow up in. I thought I knew someone who might help.

A few months earlier Eric Smith and his wife had started a Teen Challenge coffee house in a small town in the Midlands. I explained the crisis and how, somehow, Teen Challenge had to stand by Jim and show him some practical Christian love.

'How many of them are there?' Eric asked.

'Jane, two boys and a Dobermann dog. And by the way, they're black,' I added.

'Well, that'll make for an interesting situation in our rather reserved town. John, give me a chance to talk it over with my wife and family and pray about it. I'll be back in touch as soon as I can.'

Eric was as good as his word. He and his family responded rapidly and positively. 'We'll take them; they can live with us until we find them somewhere more permanent,' he promised. 'Let me know as soon as it's arranged with Jim.'

There was no doubt that this was yet another miracle. The chances of finding accommodation with a Christian family were negligible but God had done it. I couldn't wait to break the news to Jim, who had succeeded in taking his children out of care and was anxiously awaiting further news of a possible move.

'It's all arranged, Jim,' I told him triumphantly. 'Get yourselves packed and I'll take you all up to the Midlands.'

Driving into the courtyard of the block of flats in Bethnal Green I looked up and saw two young faces peering over the first-floor balcony. Suddenly the two lads started jumping up and down calling out. 'Hey Dad, the Pastor-man's here!'

Jim came to the balcony with a big grin on his face and welcomed me warmly. I walked up the stairs remembering that they were the scene of many of Jim's battles with other drug dealers; as I reached his flat several neighbours poured on to the landing to say their farewells. Jim told me later that some of them were his old drug friends.

The van was soon filled with Jim and Jane's belongings till only a couple of square feet remained at the back.

'In you get lads, and make room for the dog,' Jim said.

'Well, this is it; you're off to a new beginning,' I remarked to Jane as she climbed into the front seat beside me.

'Yes, Pastor, I hope we'll like it,' she replied rather apprehensively, as the Transit van swung out of the car park and headed north. As we passed through Hendon and on to the M1 Jane nudged Jim, and said with wonder, 'Look Jim, aren't those green fields beautiful?' Many things most people take for granted just don't exist in Bethnal Green.

After a rather eventful journey (during which the Dobermann was sick whilst we were stuck in the outside lane in a hold-up on the M1) we arrived. After four hours in such a restricted space one big Dobermann and two small boys were ready to stretch their legs. To say that Eric Smith's town was as far removed from Bethnal Green as chalk is from cheese would be an understatement. His detached house was in an elegant road with immaculate front gardens—very exciting and inviting for bored young travellers, both two-footed and four-footed varieties. I had hardly opened the rear door when the Dobermann leaped out and used the front gardens of the nearest half-dozen houses as an Aintree race-course, hotly pursued by two young lads in wellies!

Eric, having noticed our arrival—he could hardly have missed it—opened his front door to greet us. This was the signal for dog and boys to make an invasion attack on his house, to the consternation of Eric's small Scottish terrier. 'Hey Dad, this ain't half posh!' the lads said in their Cockney accents as they threw themselves on to the settee and sampled the carpets. After making the necessary introductions I felt it would be right to leave.

I drove back to Wales very tired but happy. Through the amazing grace of a pastor and his family the Lord had intervened and made a way where there seemed to be none. Within a few days Jim was back in the programme picking up where he had left off. He was more settled but by no means out of the woods. Many days of heartache and heartbreak would have to be faced before the final victory came.

One of the great strengths of a Teen Challenge programme is the quality and depth of its spiritual teaching. Most of the morning is devoted to classroom instruction; fourteen basic Bible studies make up the curriculum, together with a wide range of personal studies tailored to a student's individual needs. It was heartening to see evidence of the Holy Spirit applying the teaching to students' lives.

Bernie, from the valleys of South Wales, was as close to a madman as we were likely to meet. His search for life had taken him into every type of drug abuse, introduced him to the occult and alienated him from his family. Just weeks before entering Teen Challenge he had been in court for stealing from a local colliery: for two weeks he had driven around with a car-boot full of dynamite, intending to blow up his father's house.

After a session dealing with the principle of restitution Bernie began to show signs of uneasiness bordering on depression, and eventually decided to confide in me.

'It's what you were talking about in class the other day, Pastor. I've got a guitar at home which I stole from a club about four years ago and now I know I must give it back. The trouble is I don't know how to do it—if I get it and pack it up will you send it back to the police for me?'

'Well, that's one way of tackling it, but I'm not sure it's the right way,' I replied. 'I think you should be prepared to take it back to the police yourself and face the outcome. I know it's a hard challenge but the Lord will honour you.'

'I'll have to think about that one,' Bernie responded. 'Only a few days before I came here I was in court and at home my reputation's not very good. What if, on top of everything else, they send me down?'

Bernie was obviously going through a real spiritual crisis and finding it tough, but the teaching was bearing fruit in his life. A few days later he came back.

'I've decided I've got to do it, Pastor. I'm prepared to go back to Blackwood Police Station with the guitar, but I'd like you to come with me if you will, please.'

The Duty Sergeant at the police station recognised Bernie. 'What brings you here again?' he asked rather roughly.

'Well, ' Bernie began, 'it's a bit of unsettled business, actually. About four years ago I pinched a guitar from a club and now I've come to bring it back.'

The Sergeant looked at Bernie very strangely and left us. A few minutes later he reappeared blowing a layer of dust from the file he was carrying.

'This case was put away four years ago and would never have been re-opened. What on earth's brought you here today to confess?' the policeman asked.

'Well, sir, it's like this. Since I last saw you I've become a born-again Christian and this business has been a barrier to my spiritual progress. I know I can't go any further with the Lord until I've dealt with it. I want to make a confession and then accept whatever punishment's necessary.'

'OK,' said the policeman, 'wait there while I get the forms to take your statement.' Bernie turned to me and grinned, 'I bet he thinks I'm mad. Last time he saw me in here I had filthy long hair, dirty clothes and was drunk. Normally by now I'd have been thrown into the slammer for a few hours before they'd even see me. Things have changed a bit, eh?' he said proudly.

I looked at him and realised that they certainly had. He now looked every inch a young business executive—smart hair-style, clean shirt, suit and tie. Once again, I was looking at living proof of the grace of God.

Bernie made a full statement, had his finger-prints taken, received a standard caution and handed over the guitar. He was told the matter would be reported to the Chief Superintendent and a decision taken concerning further action. We returned to the Centre rejoicing that the Lord had given Bernie the courage to obey his Word.

A few weeks later an Inspector at Ammanford Police Station (our local police) asked me to bring Bernie for an interview. Rather apprehensively we entered his office.

'Your file has been passed to me by the Chief Superintendent of the Gwent Force following your visit to Blackwood Police Station. I've been instructed to give you an oral warning concerning the offence you committed,' the Inspector said.

'What does that mean exactly?' Bernie asked.

'Just that—it's an oral warning and no record will be kept that you committed the offence,' the Inspector explained.

The oral warning was duly delivered and for the next twenty minutes we were able to witness to this local policeman about the work God was doing in so many of the young men at the Centre. We left the police station convinced that God had used the situation to bring glory to his name, and returned to the Centre to share the good news of the way in which the Lord had honoured Bernie's faith. Such evidences of God's unfailing love were milestones to us in our developing programme.

9

The kitchen door at the Centre opened and a guy no bigger than a bag of chips cheerily announced himself in a broad Lancashire accent. 'Evening everybody, I'm Jim.' Jim had just arrived from the Induction Centre in Oxford. In his mid-twenties, he looked much older, with classic signs of heroin abuse—teeth rotted away and an underweight physique showing every symptom of hepatitis. He immediately became known as 'Little Jim', to differentiate him from 'Big Jim'.

Little Jim came from Fleetwood, Lancashire, where for the past few years he had been involved in heroin abuse, both as a user and pusher, until things got so bad he almost died.

'I'd do the most crazy things to get high,' he told me, 'because I just couldn't live without a fix. I got so desperate I'd have sold my granny to get heroin. I remember one night having nothing to fix with so I drew out my own blood and tried getting a hit with it—what a totally insane thing to do. Another time I asked my girlfriend to tie me to a lamp-post and leave me there until I'd withdrawn because I knew there was nothing I could do to help myself. The only solution I could see was a coffin. But a strange thing happened,' Jim explained, obviously pleased to relate such an interesting and powerful story.

'My girlfriend became a Christian and tried to get me converted too. It was around the time of Mission England;

Billy Graham was holding special meetings at Anfield football ground and my girlfriend persuaded me to go one night. I couldn't believe what I saw, a ground packed with people who'd come to hear a man I never knew existed. But when he began to talk it seemed as if he knew all about me, because he had a lot to say about drugs and how Christ could save and deliver drug addicts.

'I could hardly believe my ears. It was what I'd wanted to hear for a long time but I never thought there was a way out, and then suddenly this person comes all the way from America to tell me that Jesus is the way. It's amazing!' Jim paused, shaking his head and repeating again, 'It's amazing!' This, I was to learn, was one of his favourite expressions.

'When Billy Graham gave his invitation I couldn't stay in my seat and went forward with hundreds of other people. Then God performed another miracle. The guy who started to counsel me had been a drug addict himself. He knew exactly what I was going through—it was amazing! After I'd accepted the Lord I was put into contact with Fleetwood Full Gospel Church; but because I needed so much help they recommended Teen Challenge. I couldn't have stayed in Fleetwood anyway: there were too many people out to get me.'

As our Centre filled up with young men from all sorts of backgrounds and with all sorts of problems I marvelled at the atmosphere the Holy Spirit was creating among them. Our accommodation was cramped, the bedrooms housing two students were claustrophobic, and there was nowhere anyone could go to be alone. In many ways it was a classic recipe for disaster, especially in view of the former life-styles of the students who now rubbed shoulders with each other. Yet the Lord's presence prevented any violence or serious aggression ever being experienced.

Like every family we had our differences and there were times when discipline was handed out, but the recognition that we were a family always held us together in times of crisis. Nevertheless inter-personal relationships were not always problem-free. In fact difficulties sometimes arose through no fault of the parties concerned but as a product of old memories and experiences being resurrected through something a fellow student had innocently done or said.

About 8.00pm one evening I was supervising evening studies when an agitated Little Jim virtually demanded a counselling session.

'What's your problem, Jim?' I asked gently. He sat opposite me in my office with his head bowed and for a long time said nothing. Eventually he said in a low voice, 'I find myself hating one of the other students more every day even though the guy concerned is totally innocent and I shouldn't be feeling this way towards him. It's tearing me apart. I can't go on like this. One day I'll attack him.'

He was obviously in great distress. 'Jim, I don't know what's causing this problem or who the other student is, but the Lord wants to set you free from this torment tonight. If you're prepared to open up to me we can pray about it and receive the Lord's help now,' I suggested, really exercising my faith.

'It's a very personal thing, but I'm willing to share it with you,' Jim said falteringly. 'In my teens I was attacked and raped in a park by an alcoholic. He was a large man, I was helpless against him and I've felt bitter towards him ever since. Peter resembles my attacker so much that whenever I see him I keep reliving the attack and building up more resentment against Peter. I just don't know what to do, Pastor, but I can't go on any longer under this pressure.'

'Jim,' I began, 'the Lord is aware of your problem and has been wanting to comfort you ever since it happened. He will set you free if you're prepared to obey. The key to the situation is the man who attacked you. I believe the Lord will help you to forgive him tonight so that you can be immediately set free from your bitter feelings.'

'How can I forgive him after what he did? He acted like

73

an animal! He doesn't deserve to be forgiven.' Jim said with noticeable bitterness in his voice.

'Jim, think for a moment. When you came to Christ in Anfield Stadium did you deserve forgiveness? All the things you'd done to get drugs, the hurt and pain you were involved in causing—did you deserve to be forgiven, or was it God's free gift to you as part of his salvation in Jesus?'

Jim shook his head acknowledging the truth of what I was saying. I continued, 'Jim, what happened to you was horrific and I don't pretend to understand how it affected you, but it was the result of sin. God hated what that man did to you, but he still loves him as a person. If he comes to Christ tonight God will forgive him. The man who attacked you did it because sin had a hold on his life and found expression in his particular weakness. This man needs Christ and I'm asking you not only to forgive him but to pray that the Lord will save him.' Jim still sat with his head in his hands.

'Jim, if we believe that people hurt us intentionally it makes it very hard to forgive them, even though we must still do so. However, if we can believe that people hurt us in ignorance of the pain they are causing it helps us to forgive them. On the cross Jesus prayed, "Father, forgive them, because they don't know what they're doing." Very often people don't realise the pain they cause but are driven by sinful urges which dominate their whole thinking. I'm sure your attacker didn't stop to think about any lasting effect on you, and was only concerned about satisfying his lust. Does that help?' I asked.

Jim looked up and though still very obviously distressed he said, 'Yes, Pastor, that helps a lot. I want to be free of this and I believe now that my attacker abused me because of the sin in his life. It helps to remember that Jesus was abused and was prepared to forgive. I want to do the same.'

Jim started shaking as he prepared to do something that would release him from Satan's judgement and condemnation. We prayed, Jim forgiving his abuser and asking the Lord to save him, then thanking the Lord for destroying the barrier between himself and Peter and releasing him from hatred.

He looked up, relief on his face and peace in his eyes. 'It's amazing, I feel so different! God's answered my prayer. Can I go and share it with the others?' he asked eagerly, 'It's nine o'clock—study time's over.'

He ran into the lounge where the others were packing up their books. Gesturing excitedly he climbed onto the settee shouting, 'I'm free, I'm free, Jesus has set me free!' It was a wonderful moment and in the circumstances I did not have the heart to rebuke him for abusing the furniture!

As time went by Little Jim grew stronger in the Lord and was given many opportunities to share his testimony in public. It was always thrilling to hear him relate the above episode, making public a private counselling session. Incidentally, he and Peter became inseparable friends.

10

Teen Challenge is the heartbeat of God. This may seem an extravagant or unjustified claim but for those involved in the daily ministry there is no shadow of doubt about it.

Historically, the organisation began when David Wilkerson obeyed the call of God and ventured into the gang-infested streets of New York City in 1958. But in reality the work was born when Jesus himself took the scroll in the synagogue in Nazareth and read aloud the words of Isaiah, 'The Spirit of the Lord is on me, because he has anointed me to preach good news to the poor. He has sent me to proclaim freedom for the prisoners and recovery of sight for the blind, to release the oppressed, to proclaim the year of the Lord's favour.' (Luke 4:18, 19)

No one believes for a moment that God did not inspire and direct David Wilkerson when Teen Challenge was founded in those early exciting days of 1958, but in truth David did something which the church should already have been doing. In this sense Teen Challenge filled a gap in the church's ministry and ever since has been working to put itself out of business by encouraging, provoking and helping local churches to 'take on board' this ministry as a normal part of their work.

From its inception in 1958, the work of Teen Challenge has always been on a 'faith basis'. Contrary to popular belief, no finance is received from the USA to start or support new ministries and every Teen Challenge work has a financial autonomy which ensures that ministries must always proceed in faith and believe God to supply whatever is needed to fulfil the vision he gives. There are always more requests for help than we can afford to respond to. However, though money is never plentiful, God has enabled Teen Challenge ministries to open in over forty countries and it is he who sustains them all.

To some, Teen Challenge must seem like Paul's 'thorn in the flesh,' constantly niggling and reminding them of the life-controlling and life-destroying problems faced by thousands of people on their doorsteps. Even today when many churches have grown beyond what most people would have thought possible in the UK, very few are equipped to offer help to addicts or to those suffering from other behavioural problems. This is not a criticism but an observation, from which I feel it may fairly be concluded that Teen Challenge has a relevant and important contribution to make to the body of Christ for the foreseeable future.

Where local churches and Teen Challenge combine their vision and resources and work together for the common good of 'Luke 4:18 people' miracles still happen. I praise the Lord for the increasing number of churches opening to us and discovering that we are not a threat but have something positive and dynamic to contribute regardless of the size or maturity of that particular church.

For example, one Sunday evening I was preaching in Dover, Kent, and a young man obviously under great pressure sat at the back. He responded immediately to my gospel appeal and during counselling after the service I discovered he had a serious drug problem. There was absolutely no way Phil could stay in the area without continual pressure from the drug scene, and anyway the local church, live and thriving as it was, could not offer him the structured and intensive daily help that he needed. When my services were over on Tuesday night Phil returned with me to the Centre where he successfully completed our programme. That local church has always been grateful for the way Teen Challenge stepped in and offered help on behalf of the church to someone needing an extended period of spiritual rehabilitation.

In November 1984 we had our first referral from Liverpool, sometimes known as 'Smack City'. A local pastor telephoned asking whether we could assist a young man urgently seeking help. 'Bring him down as soon as you can,' I responded. 'We'll interview him here and if everything goes well he can move on to our Induction Centre immediately.'

It was Thanksgiving Day when Brian and his pastor arrived. Although our normal meals were always adequate Betty-Ruth insisted that in keeping with her American roots we should celebrate Thanksgiving Day with a banquet. Brian arrived to an evening meal of roast turkey, cranberry sauce, roasted marshmallows and, of course, pumpkin pie. He sat at our rather large dining table in a state of bewilderment—a combination of withdrawing from heroin and 'culture' shock. He was in desperate need of help and it was agreed that his Pastor would take him to Oxford the next morning.

As we gathered as usual in the student lounge at 10.00pm for evening prayers, Brian, dressed in a long black overcoat and shaking from withdrawal effects, knelt in the middle of the room. His greasy hair rested unkemptly on his shoulders and in his hands he clutched the large Bible he had brought.

'Jesus, dear Jesus, please help me,' he sobbed in his Scouse accent. 'Jesus, I'm so scared, please help me.' Our hearts went out to him as we felt helpless to do anything but assure him of our love and of the Lord's power to deliver him. That in itself was more than he had received before, and although his condition was still desperate, Brian had at least turned the corner towards recovery. It would be long and painful, but it had started.

A month later I was at the crowded Swansea bus station to meet Brian on his return from the Oxford Induction Centre. I was a few minutes late, the Oxford bus had already dropped its passengers and Brian was nowhere to be seen. I walked up and down and eventually decided to phone the Centre to see if they had heard from him. As I walked over to the kiosk I noticed a rather smart, well-groomed young man using the phone. He had his back to me but as I got nearer he turned round. I could hardly believe my eyes. He looked vaguely like Brian, but surely it couldn't be?

'Excuse me,' I asked him, 'are you Brian?'

'Yes, that's right. Thank goodness you've come; I was just phoning the Centre to find out what had happened,' he explained with a wide smile on his face.

Brian had been brought up in a working-class family plagued by drink. Both parents were alcoholics and although his father once had a successful paving business it had all collapsed because of his drink problem. In an attempt to start a new life for himself Brian had entered Naval College at 16 and was training to be a radio operator when the war in Afghanistan broke out. He had panicked and left the College, afraid that the war would spread and he would find himself caught up in it—and despite joining the Navy he couldn't even swim.

He found himself locked into a situation offering him little hope or prospects. As an unemployed youth in Liverpool he became just one of many thousands in the same boat, so anything that offered to break the monotony became of interest. Drugs gained an increasing hold on him until he was addicted to speed and was also a regular user of acid, and finally heroin.

'I used to wander around Liverpool like Little Boy Blue, completely stoned and with a blue and white mohican hair-style—the colours of Everton football club. One of my main interests was drawing and I became quite good at it—in fact, the Peace Movement spotted one of my posters and asked me to do some work for them. I was searching for reality, meaning, something to live for, so it wasn't long before I became a full-time member of the organisation. At least at the time I thought I was doing something useful although now I can see how pointless it was and how foolish I must have seemed to normal people. There I was, dressed like a punk, drugged to the eyeballs and proclaiming "Make Love, Not War!" I guess really, deep down inside, I was looking for love, and God used the Peace Movement to reach me. He knew I was lost and lonely and he came right to where I was. Do you want to hear about it?' he asked.

'I certainly do! You never know, one day I might write a book about you all,' I joked.

'Well,' Brian took a deep breath and launched into an account of his conversion. 'We'd decided to hold a Peace Festival and it was my job to look after some of the publicity and organise some of the campsites. One night as I walked around I saw a small tent that shouldn't have been there because it hadn't booked in. I went to investigate and was completely taken aback when I read what was written outside it: "Come and meet the Prince of Peace". I looked at the tent and the little guy sitting outside, as if I was seeing things; then I asked, "Hey mate, are you the Prince of Peace?"

"No," he replied, "but if you'd like to step inside I'll introduce you to him."

'By now my curiosity was uncontrollable and you can imagine how let-down I felt when I saw no one in the tent. Then my new friend told me about Jesus and for the first time in my life I heard the truth I'd been searching for. I don't think I became a Christian that night but we prayed together and I left with a strange feeling inside. Something was beginning to happen.

'A couple of nights later I found myself at a typical drug-scene party. We'd all get high and pretend we'd had a good time but somehow I couldn't get into the mood. After a while a girl with lovely blonde hair asked me to go outside with her and since this normally meant only one thing I agreed. I still can't believe what happened next: instead of putting her arms round me she looked me straight in the eye and said, "Brian, you need Jesus in your life." I couldn't believe what I was hearing right there in the drug party. It scared me so much I burst into tears and left.

'My one thought was to find Tommy, my Prince of Peace friend, and ask him for his help. I remembered he'd said he lived in Toxteth. I'd no idea where and Toxteth is quite a big place, but in my desperation I was sure God would lead me to him. I jumped on a Toxteth bus not knowing really where I was going, just hoping for another miracle. As the bus drove down one of the main streets in Toxteth I suddenly saw it again, "Come and meet the Prince of Peace". I knew God had answered my prayer and guided me to the man who could help me. Tommy led me to the Lord and I was born again. During the next couple of days he took me to a fellowship in Devonshire Road who got in touch with you. By the way, the girl who spoke to me at the party turned out to be Tommy's cousin! She's backslidden now, but the Lord still used her to get through to me. What do you think of that, Pastor?'

'Well, Brian, as Little Jim would say, "It's amazing!" '

We were only weeks away from our first Teen Challenge Christmas and it was interesting to watch the lads reacting to what, for them, would be a new experience. For some a sober Christmas was hard to imagine and it would be the first time any of them had celebrated its true meaning. As food parcels, money and dozens of presents arrived the lads were overawed at the kindness that churches and individual Christians were showing them.

Christmas Eve was much the same as in any other house full of children. Our lads were far from childhood but as dishes of nuts, sweets and chocolates, and bottles of pop and squash were placed around the beautifully decorated lounge it was as if many of them went backwards in a time machine.

'Man,' Brian said, 'I've never seen anything like this before. All we ever had in our house at Christmas were bottles of booze!' He dug into the sweets and chocolates as if there was no tomorrow.

'Last Christmas I was on my own and had baked beans on toast for dinner. I'm going to enjoy this one!' said Peter.

At midnight an attempt was made to get everyone to bed so that the final touches could be put to preparing the scene for the morning but even at 1.30am some were still trying to sneak down to see what was happening—the excitement factor was running very high! Literally dozens of presents were piled high against the tree and Christmas stockings—ten in all, one for each student—hung from the snooker table.

For some the sight of the present-bedecked lounge on Christmas morning was too much to take and they found great difficulty in hiding their emotions.

'Pastor,' Little Jim said to me very seriously, 'can I see you in your office, please?' A counselling session on Christmas morning was the last thing I had planned but obviously something was on Jim's mind.

'Pastor, this is all too much for me. All those presents out there, I just can't take all this kindness; it's cracking me up!' he confessed.

The Christmas holidays had brought a relaxation to our tight daily schedule but had also served to highlight the need for our structured programme. The suspension of the daily timetable showed how difficult most of the lads found it to organise their own affairs and it was with a sigh of relief from everyone that we settled back into our normal routine.

11

Probably the greatest shock to the system that those entering our programme suffer is getting up at 7.15am each morning and engaging in meaningful work each afternoon. A drug habit affects body, mind, and especially the will, which is ultimately destroyed. Addicts are therefore very unpredictable, with thought-patterns and attitudes conditioned to thinking only about the need for drugs and how to get them. The will to do anything else has been completely eroded and drug addiction, far from being a pleasurable pastime, becomes an occupation. Drugs are no longer taken to give 'high' or pleasurable feelings but must be used at regular intervals simply to prevent an addict from becoming sick. Getting drugs becomes the number one priority and everything and everyone else must take second place. I remember Big Jim once explaining to me the horrors of a drug addict's 'occupation'.

'Every night before I went to sleep I had to make sure I had my fix ready for the morning because without it I was going to be very sick. The first thing I did on waking was use the fix and then I knew I had only so many hours to find my next one. If I had no money I had to get some; that meant shop-lifting, breaking into cars or generally hustling to get some buying power. Stolen articles had to be sold so I was faced with the added problem of selling them in a pub. This took more time and involved more risk with the count-down for my next fix getting nearer to zero all the time.

'Having got the money I then had to locate my supplier and sometimes I'd discover he'd been busted by the police. That might mean a journey across London to find another one with time running out fast. Once I'd got my junk I'd rush home, dash into the bathroom and shoot up. A sense of euphoria would sweep over me and I'd spend the afternoon flat out on my bed. The next day it would be the same thing all over again, and then again, and again.'

It was obvious that if the lads coming into our programme were to find employment on leaving, we had to make them employable. Most had never worked and, with a few exceptions, considered work a four-letter word. Even if we could not teach them marketable skills we realised that an essential part of our practical training must involve changing their attitudes towards work— including responding positively to authority, working under supervision, and working to consistently high standards. For us to achieve this it was important to simulate realistic working conditions of the kind the lads might reasonably be expected to encounter after leaving the programme.

To fulfil these objectives we decided to concentrate our activities on two main areas; firstly, building maintenance work and secondly, craft manufacturing. In March 1985 a 'Starter Factory Unit' was rented from the Carmarthen District Council for the latter. Students with an aptitude for such work then had to apply themselves at a work bench for three hours each afternoon to produce scripture prints, framed pictures, wall plaques and clocks to sell at the different churches we visited. It was constructive, rewarding work and gave a great deal of job satisfaction, which was reflected in an increased sense of self-worth.

This workshop later provided paid employment for at least four graduates from our programme and was an essential step in enabling them to proceed to better-paid and more attractive situations. In September 1986 a second factory unit was obtained as our work programme began to expand.

The first objective—providing a building maintenance programme—was less easy to realise because of the limited amount of maintenance work available within the lads' capabilities. Within weeks, however, all that changed.

In early 1985 it was clear that the Induction Centre at Oxford was not paying its way. In fact it was getting more and more into debt each month. This was due to several factors, not least high rents in the city of Oxford. In April it was finally decided to close it, but since an Induction Centre was still a top priority it became urgently necessary to find suitable new accommodation, preferably near our main Centre. This would not be easy since funds were low and we had no financial credibility or collateral with which to borrow money. We had to find a property needing renovation to use as a building work project and thus save ourselves a considerable sum. Where, I thought time and time again, was such a building?

Then out of the blue one of the staff asked, 'Have you seen that old vicarage on the way to our factory unit? It's a big house; maybe it's just the thing we're looking for!'

Although I had passed the house at least twice a day for over six weeks, I had never noticed it. It sounded as if it could be the place, and a superficial external examination aroused our interest. Built in 1893, and set in its own grounds, the fine old house had obviously seen better days but still retained much of its character. Potentially it offered the perfect solution to our problem except for one small detail: we had no money. The house had been empty for three or four years, the last vicar having left it because of excessive damp problems, and was to be sold by auction during the first week in May—now just a matter of weeks away. We rejoiced, knowing there were no coincidences with God—only, as one student used to say, God-incidences.

At this time I received a rather unusual telephone call

from a lady in London who had heard that we were looking for a new Induction Centre. 'The Lord has prompted me to telephone you because he's told me that you will have your new Centre. I'm not a crank or spiritual nutcase but I do often receive a word from the Lord about specific things. In fact,' she continued, 'the Lord has given me a vision of what the house looks like. It's in rather bad condition and will need a lot of work done on it. Am I making any sense to you?'

'Well, we have seen an old house that generally meets with your description,' I admitted, feeling fairly sceptical. 'It's a nice old house, very welcoming and homely inside; it used to be a vicarage,' I added.

My friend in London seemed taken aback at this and continued in a more subdued tone, 'Well, we can't possibly be talking about the same property; there must be another one the Lord has for you since mine has a sort of barn at the back. Vicarages just don't have barns,' she concluded, sounding rather disappointed.

'Hang on a minute,' I replied, getting more excited myself now, 'at the back of this vicarage there is a sort of barn. Behind the house there's a coach house and stable which could very easily be mistaken for a barn.'

'That's it then,' she shouted down the phone, 'that confirms it; the Lord's going to give it to you.'

A few days later she phoned again. 'I've been praying about the house you were talking about and I asked the Lord to give me a verse of scripture to confirm my vision. The verse I keep getting is Deuteronomy 32:13 [AV]; in that, there's the phrase "the high places of the earth". I believe the Lord's telling me the house you're to have is on a hill. Is it?'

I was amazed, because whilst the village of Gorslas is generally flat, the house in question is on a hill and visible from virtually everywhere in the locality! The Lord was graciously giving us further encouragement, but there was still one detail that concerned me. Where was the money to come from?

The auction was scheduled for the first week in May, an unfortunate date because I would be attending a ministers' conference in Bradford. Ken would be busy overseeing the programme so it was agreed that Clive Evans would attend the sale to bid on Teen Challenge's behalf.

'We have to pay a deposit of 10% of the sale price to the auctioneer, Clive, so I don't think we can bid above £27,500. We've got just £2,800 in the bank, so if you put 10% down we'll have virtually nothing left over. We'll certainly have to trust God for our day-to-day needs then,' I advised him. The only reason the house would sell for such a low sum was its poor condition, a fact which I hoped would deter other people.

On the day of the sale I could hardly wait for the conference in Bradford to end. The house had to be ours—but was it? I phoned the Centre and spoke to Clive.

'Hello, John, you've got yourself a vicarage,' he announced.

'Praise the Lord!' I responded. 'What happened?'

'There was quite a bit of interest, but as the bidding got into the £20,000 bracket it ended up with just me and someone else. We kept bidding against each other until he offered £27,000. I knew our limit was £27,500 so I made my last bid. Miraculously nobody opposed it. I put the £2,750 down and you have six weeks to find the balance.'

'Well, thank God we've got the house, but it leaves us a bit short in the bank, doesn't it?' I concluded.

'It's not as bad as you think, John. I've got more good news for you. In this morning's post was a cheque for £1,000 from Lancashire with a note saying "I hope it arrives in time for the auction", and someone else came up with a £500 gift in the auction itself so we've had two miracles today!'

During the next fortnight further gifts more than covered the deposit placed on the house at the auction. We were so grateful to the Lord for these signs of his faithfulness and love but at the back of my mind was the fact that we had only a month to find another £22,000—or lose our deposit.

These were testing times for our faith but I was enjoying every moment. As the days slipped by however I began to sense that the Lord was not going to supply the remaining money as a 'gift from heaven'. It was as if he was asking us to put our faith on the line in a way which might even involve our personal security and reputation. I made an appointment with the Centre's bank manager. After outlining the situation I finally came out with my request: 'I need £22,000 urgently!' I said, looking him straight in the eye.

To my amazement he left his desk and announced to his chief clerk, 'I'm going out to view a property with Mr Macey. I'll be back in about an hour.'

As I drove to meet him at the old vicarage I felt very apprehensive. I hadn't expected such a quick response and what if he didn't like what he saw? After all, it was in a very bad state of repair and one had to have a fair amount of imagination to see it in its full glory after renovations were completed. What if he wanted a surveyor's report? These and other questions were buzzing around in my mind as I walked up the drive to meet him outside the old house.

Bank managers are shrewd men and usually fairly non-committal unless they are confident that all the conditions are in their favour. As we walked around the house he exchanged pleasantries with me but my heart was sinking a bit as I began to see the building through 'natural' eyes. There were signs of dry rot, plaster was falling from walls because of damp, and everywhere was badly in need of modernising and decorating. Most of the external walls needed hacking off and replastering, windows needed replacing and the grounds were completely overgrown.

Sensing that perhaps there would be some reluctance on his part to advance any money against this house I said rather nervously, 'I know there's a lot to be done, but if you need some extra security my wife and I will stand as guarantors.' Just a few weeks earlier the Lord had miraculously arranged for us to move into our own bungalow through the generosity of Christian friends. Although a considerable sum had been loaned to us privately the deeds were with the bank. My offer obviously impressed the bank manager because he stopped in his tracks and said, 'You really believe in this project, don't you?'

'Of course,' I assured him, 'otherwise I wouldn't be wasting your time or mine.'

'Well,' he began, 'I don't know very much about Teen Challenge or whether you'll be able to raise the income to pay the loan but I do believe in you. I'm willing to back you as a person and I don't think it will be necessary to accept your offer of a personal guarantee. Go ahead and sign the cheque to complete your purchase of this property.'

God had performed another miracle. The transaction was duly completed by using the bank's overdraft facilities but then came a nasty shock. When the bank's solicitors checked the trust deed of Teen Challenge they discovered that the charity was not empowered to borrow money for the purpose of buying property. Since the deal had already been completed this caused the bank manager considerable embarrassment and necessitated his calling Ann and myself into his office.

'I'm sorry about all this,' he apologised, 'but it seems we've jumped the gun a bit. There's only one way round it: you will have to act as guarantors for the overdraft. Will you sign these papers please?' As we left the bank we looked at each other both thinking the same thing. We were now completely reliant on the Lord to provide for the loan to be paid or we might find ourselves homeless again.

Incidentally, we later learned that after an audit, the bank inspectors ruled that even an overdraft was not permissible according to the Teen Challenge trust deed. It seemed that legally and humanly speaking there was no way we should have been allowed to borrow the money, but God 'who rules in the affairs of men' had given us favour with the right bank manager at the right time.

The old vicarage, quickly renamed 'The White House', provided Ken with a challenge which he relished. He set some of the lads to work on the grounds, cutting back years of jungle growth whilst others tackled the hundred and one other jobs that needed doing. As Ken instructed them in hacking off the external walls and exposing the interior ones to tackle the problem of damp we soon realised that we had bought more than we had bargained for. The house had its fair share of dry rot, wet rot, and goodness knows what. Major beams needed replacing, wooden lintels were replaced by steel girders and whole floors had to be relaid. Damp courses were inserted and finally the whole house was redecorated.

There are no coincidences with God, and it was not by chance that whilst all this work was taking place we received our youngest referral, a lad called Tom. Though only 16 he had become involved in drug abuse and came to us following a massive overdose which almost killed him.

His parents, both Christians, had brought him to the Centre with his close friend, David Ellis. The Lord who knows all things had directed Tom to Teen Challenge for us to help him, but he had also brought David Ellis to us for him to help us. An experienced plasterer and general builder, he was just the man we needed but could not afford. Soon David and Tom's father were working flat out plastering both the inside and outside of the White House as a service for God. Such kindness and dedication by the Lord's people always left an indelible impression on both students and staff, and encouraged us to keep going through difficult times.

By November the White House was ready to open as the new Induction Centre, with Bernard and Val, who had moved from Oxford, firmly established in the first-floor flat.

12

As well as experiencing great answers to prayer and learning to grow in faith in material and financial matters, we had always to keep before us the paramount importance of the needs of our students. We constantly reminded ourselves that nothing must be allowed to come before our ministry to the young men God had entrusted to us— they were our reason for existence. So alongside our strenuous programme and developing craft work we zealously maintained our schedule of Bible teaching each morning and regular personal counselling sessions. All counselling was on a one-to-one basis, in accordance with scriptural principles, and was never allowed to develop into group counselling sessions as frequently happens in secular programmes.

Because of the nature of the problems being dealt with it was understandable that confrontational counselling far outweighed pastoral counselling, and it amazed me how readily the lads accepted what was often a head-on approach to their unacceptable behaviour or attitudes.

Of all the students in our programme Brian was probably the most temperamental and in many ways the most difficult to handle. He frequently suffered from 'flashbacks' which left him totally confused and paranoiac and meant he needed handling with kid gloves and tremendous patience. It was painful to see his high degree of insecurity which often resulted in great spiritual depressions where he felt God had left him and that he would never be able to live the Christian life. For weeks Brian was my shadow, constantly seeking reassurance and support. When, during one such bout of depression I was nowhere to be found, he just 'vaporised'.

About 7.00pm one Monday in June after his washing-up duty Brian came looking for me for more spiritual help. Unfortunately I had just left. This threw him into total panic and he did what he knew best—he ran. Taking nothing with him he disappeared into thin air and although we searched for hours he was nowhere to be found. It was the following Friday before we heard any news of him, when the DHSS in Bristol telephoned to verify the facts he had given them on his new claim to benefit. I was overjoyed to learn that he was safe and alive and all I wanted to do was to speak to him.

'Please ask him to phone me,' I pleaded with the clerk. 'Just tell him that he's welcome to come back.'

At 6.00pm that evening Brian telephoned, tearfully asking us to forgive him and to consider taking him back, which we immediately agreed to do. By 8.00pm Ann and I were in Bristol where we met a very subdued, not to mention dirty and smelly Brian. The next morning after a bath and a good night's sleep Brian was ready to tell his story.

'Honestly, Pastor, I didn't want to go. I really do love the Lord and I want to serve him, but when I couldn't find you I panicked. I was having one of my bad times and I couldn't think straight. All I wanted was space to try and sort myself out, so I ran down the hill and all the way into Ammanford [some five miles] because I knew you'd go looking for me in the other direction. I then got a lift to London. The strange thing is that although I was running away I witnessed to the lorry driver who picked me up and in the end he told me I should get out and go back to Teen Challenge. Of course I didn't and early Tuesday morning I was in Leicester Square, hungry, tired and frightened.

'I wandered around for quite a while and then found

myself praying, "Please Lord, send a Christian to help me!" I opened my eyes and the next person I saw was wearing a Christian badge, so I stopped him and asked him to help me. It's amazing; I know the Lord was with me because this fellow took me to his home in Wimbledon where his mother gave me a meal and the bus fare for me to catch the overnight coach to Liverpool. So Wednesday morning I arrived in my old home city, very tired.

'As I wandered around all my old haunts I didn't feel I belonged there any more. My feet were killing me so I sat dangling them in the river for a while before I hit the road again out of Liverpool. Next morning I was in Plymouth but when I got there I thought, "What on earth am I doing here?" and immediately looked for another lift which took me back to Bristol. I spent Thursday night sleeping in some cardboard boxes under bushes in a park. That's why I ponged so badly when you picked me up—I hadn't washed for five days!

'On Friday I met another junkie from Liverpool and I witnessed to him about the Lord. He'd read *The Cross and the Switchblade* and although he'd never found Christ for himself he thought I should get back to Teen Challenge as soon as possible. The girls in the DHSS office told me that you wanted me to phone you and when I told my friend this he encouraged me to do it. "You're lucky somebody cares about you," he said. So I phoned you, and oh boy, am I glad I did!' So were we all.

When our programme first started we were all super-cautious, conscious that we were living in a generally hostile community where people were just waiting for something to go wrong so that they could criticise our work. One of the safeguards we had laid down was that before coming a lad must have been drug-free for at least a month and must also have committed his life to the Lord. As the years have passed and our experience and confidence have grown this rule has often been relaxed. In the early days it was impossible to stop one or two slipping through the net without meeting these conditions and on reflection I am sure the Lord enabled them to do so.

One of these was Colin from Islington, who had been referred to us by a youth worker, Nick Adams. Colin and a friend had asked Nick to help them get out of London to have a chance to beat their serious heroin problem. When they arrived for an interview Colin appeared uninterested whilst his friend was all for joining the programme, but a few days later it was Colin who set out from London.

He was a good-looking young man, with a winning smile, and an appealing Cockney accent. His life, however, bore many of the scars common to all those in the programme, except that Colin had also suffered the pain of seeing both his parents die, his mother just the previous Christmas. Following her death his drug problem had got worse until he knew he must do something about it before it was too late. Nick Adams, the youth worker at his local Anglican church, was the only person Colin really respected and trusted.

'Nick's a good guy,' Colin told me, 'he always does his best for guys like me and I knew he'd do everything possible to help me.' Colin's only experience of the church had been through its youth club, and though he had always considered himself a Christian he discovered soon after his arrival at our Centre that this was not the case. He shared a room with Brian who could be relied on to give him all the help he needed to settle in. But Colin did not find it easy, despite making a decision to receive the Lord into his life within his first few days at the Centre. I found myself involved in two to three hour counselling sessions with him.

'Pastor, I just can't settle here; I feel so homesick for London. I'm not a country boy; I've lived for years on the streets and I miss them terribly. I must go back. I'm sure I won't start using again now I've decided to give it up.' Every day for the first three weeks he would repeat the same things and I would spend the next two or three hours pointing out that the devil was trying to deceive him, and that once back in London he would find that nothing had changed. Eventually Colin would respond by saying, 'OK, Pastor, you've won today, but I'll be going tomorrow.' The next day we would go through the same process and the miracle was that Colin stayed.

Weeks later I discovered that his main reason for staying was not my persuasive arguments but something far more convincing—the power of God. He had come to us still using heroin but of course once in our programme that had stopped. He waited for his withdrawal symptoms to start, the sweats, running nose, aches and stomach cramps but amazingly they never came. Each night Brian had prayed with him and the Lord had answered. Colin was mystified, unable to believe what was happening to him because he had tried many times to go 'cold turkey' when he was in London, but had always given in to the powerful withdrawal pains and gone back to using again.

His experience began to prove to him that God was in the Centre and despite the fact that he couldn't understand the how's or why's he couldn't deny that something good was happening to him. Despite everything however, I never felt truly happy that Colin was settled. There still seemed to be a restlessness about him. I was sure he was saved but I suspected that he still yearned for certain aspects of his old life.

A few weeks later a crisis developed which became a turning point for him. A strictly enforced rule at the Centre is that all incoming mail is opened in front of the addressee and though the mail is not read, the envelope and its contents are inspected—for obvious reasons. One day a letter arrived simply addressed to 'Teen Challenge Centre'. I opened it with the rest of the day's mail and immediately realised it was intended for Colin. I could not stop my eyes wandering over the first page because even the opening line was full of obscenity and was an obvious inducement from an old friend for Colin to return to London. As I read I became more and more disturbed by the nature of the temptations so vividly described which could have had a dramatically destructive effect on Colin.

I put the letter to one side, not knowing how to deal with the situation. On the one hand it seemed God had made it possible for me to intercept the letter, but on the other hand, how would Colin react if he found out that I had not passed on a letter which was obviously meant for him? It was a perplexing dilemma because I so desperately wanted to build up a relationship of trust and respect with him but I also wanted to shelter him from an obvious satanic attack. The day passed and I still hadn't given him the letter, but the more I thought and prayed about it the more I became convinced that I would have to. I had to trust God to help Colin see this was a deliberate move by the enemy to seduce him.

The next day I called Colin into my office and held up the envelope and letter which had arrived the day before. 'Colin, this letter came yesterday, and as you can see it was not addressed to anyone in particular so I opened it. I discovered it was meant for you and I must tell you that I found myself reading it. I have to confess I'm shocked by its contents. It's obviously from one of your old mates, and if you take my advice you'll let me tear it up without you reading it.'

He was obviously taken aback and his initial reaction was hostile. 'You'd no right to read the letter when you saw it was meant for me,' he protested. 'You've invaded my privacy and I don't know whether I can trust you any more!'

This was just the reaction I had dreaded. I tried to pacify him. 'But Colin, can't you see that the Lord is in this? Out of all the letters you get, it's this one that wasn't addressed to you—I'm sure he wanted me to read it so that I can help you see it for what it is—a trap.'

'I don't care about that; you're the man of God so I suppose you know about these things. I just want my letter, please. After I've read it I'll let you know whether I'm going to stay.' He went off to his room and I sensed he was about to embark on a great spiritual battle, one young man against the powers of darkness. There was nothing anyone could do, except pray.

A few days later Colin knocked on my door. 'I've had a long time to think about that letter and I've made my decision,' he announced. 'You've probably guessed that for quite a while I've been unsettled. I can't forget some of the things I've given up to come here. It's really been worrying me and this letter brings it to a sort of a head, doesn't it? Well, I've thought about it and even done some praying. It's got to be one thing or the other and I've decided I don't belong out there any more. The Lord's showed me that it's all rubbish and although one part of me still finds it tempting I know I've got something much better here. I've decided that I'm all out for Jesus; now you can tear up the letter!'

My heart leapt for joy as I realised that Colin had come through to victory with no human assistance. We hugged each other and thanked the Lord for his triumph in Colin's life.

'Oh, and by the way,' Colin said as he turned to go, 'I'm sorry for the way I spoke to you the other day!'

13

I was sitting in the plush impressive office of one of Britain's most senior politicians. For several years he had been a member of Her Majesty's Government and on hearing of our new work amongst young people with drug problems had expressed an interest and invited me to discuss our project with him. After digesting the sheaf of information I had presented to him he looked up with a rather puzzled expression and said,

'I don't quite understand this. I mean, all these people,'—he pointed to the page giving details of our personnel—'if they don't get paid how on earth do you manage to recruit them? I've heard the expression, "The Lord will provide", but I'd like to know how you managed to obtain the services of so many excellently qualified people.'

I smiled and with some satisfaction replied, 'Well, you've already answered your own question. The Lord really does provide!'

Next to finance, finding the right staff has always been our main challenge. As the work expanded the need for extra personnel became more urgent but we were always caught in the same trap—we needed the best but could afford to pay very little. We had had to spend much of our income on equipment, a vehicle for transporting the students and, of course, buying and renovating the White House. There was little left over to pay staff! It was not surprising, therefore, that such a question should be asked in the light of our highly qualified and experienced work force. The Lord had motivated men and women to help us who were able to command high salaries in other fields but who had heard the call of God to help mend troubled young lives. Although we could never boast of being overstaffed, the Lord's sense of timing was spot on, when it came to providing new staff!

As the time drew near for Ken's retirement we were very conscious that special people would be needed to replace him and Betty. They had set a wonderful example in the way they had dedicated themselves to setting up the programme and I knew that they would be sorely missed. Although they had to make their plans for retirement they did not want to leave the Centre until replacements had been found.

'If you mean that, I think you'll be here forever, Ken,' I joked, because he would be extremely difficult to replace. His spiritual maturity and unflappable temperament had made him ideal for a founder role. Betty's administrative, medical and all-round abilities would be sorely missed but I knew it would be wrong to try to persuade them to stay. They had done more than anyone could have asked of them and they thoroughly deserved a more leisurely life-style. I was naturally concerned about how we would manage, but I need not have worried because the Lord had it all in hand. Though I didn't know it he had been working in the hearts of another dedicated couple who applied to join us at the Centre on a voluntary basis.

Don and Gwyneth Harding had been members of my congregation in Brynmawr, Gwent and with a sense of great joy I welcomed them onto our staff team. Don was admirably suited to working alongside the lads in practical situations and was also able to offer them a lot of spiritual encouragement. Gwyneth, a real work-horse, managed to get through a tremendous amount of practical work including washing and cleaning and everything else that needed to be done. Another added blessing was David

Ellis's decision to join our Centre as a staff member and although he was still only in his early twenties when he arrived in April 1986 he made a first-class replacement for Ken.

The growing craft workshop needed constant supervision for which the Lord provided John Collier and his wife Elaine. Since Tim had left to get married a couple of months earlier John and David began to share the duties normally undertaken by the single staff members. There was still one major staff problem, however, to which there seemed to be no immediate solution, but again the Lord had it all under control.

Betty's departure had meant that Ann was left to try to cope with the housekeeping, accounts and secretarial work, which was obviously impossible longterm. But where would we find another first-class cook or secretary who was spiritually mature and prepared to work for a nominal wage?

Then Pauline Dunne asked whether Teen Challenge had any secretarial vacancies. The events leading up to Pauline's request were quite amazing since in 1985 she had moved to Penygroes when the missionary office of the Apostolic Church had been relocated from Bradford. For a variety of reasons Pauline had not settled in the new offices and felt the Lord was leading her to Teen Challenge, where she immediately settled in as my secretary. 'Just think, Pauline,' I often joked, 'the Lord had to make a church move its missionary headquarters just so that you could work at Teen Challenge!'

Ken and Betty's departure in April 1986 meant that for the first time since the programme started I was left with sole responsibility for the day-to-day running of the Centre. Although Clive Evans was still on our teaching staff he intended finishing in July along with Dr John Howells and Pastor Bill Lyons who were both moving away from South Wales. These losses of key staff caused me considerable concern, but again the Lord was preparing the right man to share the increasing responsibilities.

For several months Gareth Cheedy, pastor of Calvary Baptist Church, Swansea had been helping in the Centre as a part-time teacher. Gradually the Lord convinced him and his wife Pam that he wanted them to serve him in Teen Challenge full time. Gareth was ideally suited for our ministry, both spiritually and professionally. Before entering the ministry he had been a nurse, obtaining general and mental nursing qualifications, both of which would be invaluable to us. However, he and Pam had two small daughters and the family lived in a church manse.

'Gareth, come and join us! You know it's what the Lord's telling you to do,' I would badger him nearly every week.

'Hang on now, John,' he would reply, 'you must remember that I'm a staid Baptist, not a get-up-and-go Pentecostal! You must have patience with me.'

However, although Gareth had still not made up his mind it was obvious that the Lord knew he would come and in a very remarkable way he began to prepare the way.

Bernard and Val, who had been running our Induction Centre, had felt that they should leave Teen Challenge at the end of June 1986. They had given everything they had to the very demanding induction work but without extra help felt unable to continue. In view of this it was decided that the Induction Centre as such must close and its programme be amalgamated with our main programme. So what was to be done with the White House, which had housed the Induction Centre since its move from Oxford? Out of the blue in that month I was contacted by the Environmental Health Officer of Carmarthen District Council inviting me to meet him at the White House.

I was curious to know why this officer from the local council wished to see me, but when he explained I was flabbergasted!

'Last week there was a meeting of the Carmarthen

District Council at which some councillors publicly recognised the good work that Teen Challenge is doing in Gorslas. The feeling of the meeting was that something should be done to help your organisation and the Council passed a minute offering Teen Challenge three conversion grants.'

'Well, this is a turn-up for the books,' I laughed. 'I never expected this day would come.'

'It seems that you have some influential supporters on the Council, Mr Macey,' the Environmental Officer replied.

'I'm pleased to hear it, but you can be sure that this was a spontaneous gesture on their part. I've never asked them to help us,' I explained, 'but I'm sure we'll take advantage of the offer and submit plans for three units.' This, I realised, would solve some pressing staff accommodation problems.

David Ellis could hardly believe his ears when I broke the news to him. 'Hey, Dave,' I announced, 'the Council's going to pay for us to convert the White House into three flats—that'll keep you and the boys busy for a while!'

'Hallelujah, when can we start?' It was a typical response—David was always more than enthusiastic to get his teeth into a new project.

In no time at all the plans were passed and David began organising the new venture. At times like these Don Harding was a tower of strength both physically, spiritually and in his cheerful disposition. He possessed the stickability essential when it came to drilling holes through eighteen-inch stone walls! The White House conversion was a big undertaking since it involved digging up and laying new concrete floors, installing new ceilings, bathrooms and kitchens in three flats, new central heating installations and a complete rewiring, besides a host of more minor tasks. Finally we had to strip the roof and reslate it as well as dismantling the very large chimneys.

If we had ever doubted our ability to sustain a building project for the lads those doubts were now well and truly laid to rest. We were up to our necks in something that would test our abilities to the limit, but all the lads involved in the project seemed to thoroughly enjoy it. Colin, in particular, discovered to his amazement that he had an aptitude for bricklaying and began to realise that he could pursue this skill on completing the programme.

As the end of 1986 approached it was encouraging to see how, despite the turnover in our staff team, the Lord had already prepared his replacements, and we were able to face a new year with a full staff complement. Gareth and Pam were finally convinced that the Lord was leading them into Teen Challenge and began to set things in motion to join us. We all admired them for being prepared to follow God's will, especially as it meant that their two girls would need to attend a Welsh-speaking school and neither Gareth nor Pam knew a word of the language. They moved into one of the new flats in the White House. The words of that cabinet minister had proved true once again, and 'the Lord had provided'.

14

Despite the comings and goings of staff and an increased work programme, it was vital to maintain the spiritual input of the programme. The teaching continued each morning and God's Word continued to have its cleansing and life-changing impact on our students' lives. I often reminded them of the opportunity God had given in opening the door for them to come to Teen Challenge.

'I've seen guys grow more spiritually in twelve months in Teen Challenge than in five years in some of the churches I've pastored,' I would tell them. 'The Lord has taken what the devil did to destroy you and used it as a qualification to come into the best programme in the world!'

By mid-1986 several lads had successfully completed the programme, including Paul, Phil, Bernie, Peter and Brian. Bernie and Paul, our first graduates, returned to their home towns whilst Phil and Brian were employed in our Craft Unit. Peter continued at the Centre after graduation to receive further teaching.

Big Jim had made steady progress despite many domestic problems and pressures. An intelligent man, he had no problems absorbing the daily teaching programme, including the memorising of scripture verses. God had given him an insatiable appetite for his Word and it often became embarrassing for his teachers when Jim could quote chapter and verse better than anyone, themselves included.

His graduation was fixed for May and he was looking forward to being reunited with Jane and the boys. Since they had been in the Midlands they had needed to move out from Eric Smith's family so as to be eligible for council accommodation, and had to spend at least six months in the council's emergency homeless unit. This was little more than a slum dwelling shared by two or three homeless families.

'Pastor, it's not fit for animals to live in, let alone my kids. They've got all sorts of unsavoury characters coming and going,' said Jim, describing the conditions under which his family were living, 'and it's quite common to see rats running around. On my last weekend out I didn't feel like coming back to the Centre, but there's nothing I can do to help. I know I must make it here before I can ever be a proper husband or father, but I do feel guilty. They need what I'm getting here and compared with them I'm living in luxury.'

Jim was obviously under intense pressure and I admired his refusal to give in. I also felt a great respect for Eric Smith and his wife who continued to give Jane as much support as possible, though very little could take away the hardship of living in such accommodation.

As Jim's graduation drew nearer his spirits rose. The council had given Jane a comfortable semi-detached house, and wedding plans were already made for her and Jim. At last everything was coming together for them and the future looked bright. In October Ann and I had the privilege of attending their wedding which we still consider one of the highlights of our ministry in Teen Challenge. Little Jim was also at the wedding, confident and happy, in fact brimming over with enthusiasm for the Lord and enjoying every moment of his new life.

It was always good to see those who were making it in the programme and of course doubly good to monitor the progress of those who had graduated. But they represented just under half the lads accepted, and whilst by secular standards our results were outstanding it was always sad to see someone walk out of the programme. Reasons given for leaving were varied but usually boiled down to the same thing: a student's refusal to face up to his rebellion and selfishness and an insistence on having his own way.

It was interesting to observe the behaviour of those building up to leaving: they wanted to go, but hoped someone in authority would make the decision. Consequently their behaviour would often become anti-social, disruptive or simply rebellious. This would make a counselling session necessary—all part of the plan. When challenged about his unacceptable behaviour or attitude the student would complain of being picked on and suggest it might be better if he left. This was the crucial point, where the choice of words on the part of the counsellor was all-important. The offending student was usually waiting for a response which would justify his leaving, so that he would have someone to blame for yet another failure, another rejection. 'It wasn't me; they kicked me out; they're no different from anyone else,' he wanted to be able to say.

It had to be made clear that the student in question was not being asked to leave, and that whatever decision he made, he must accept responsibility for the consequences. He would then be given time to go and pray and think about his course of action.

The fact that a lad is free to leave our programme as soon as he wants to do so is an important fundamental principle. It is the answer to any charge that we are involved in brain-washing. It is very difficult to brain-wash a person who is constantly encouraged to exercise his free will and choose whether or not to accept the truth presented to him.

The drug problem in Britain has spread throughout the nation, but the major concentration of addiction is usually found in the large cities. Statistically Scotland heads the league, mainly because of the horrific drug abuse in Glasgow and Edinburgh. In early 1987 we began to receive referrals from Glasgow and as a consequence strong links were established between Teen Challenge and Christians in that city who were concerned about the growing problem. In particular the Lord burdened Bob Sievwright to reach out to these needy young people. Although Bob had tried to initiate positive action amongst local Christians it had never got off the ground, so he considered another project, this time with Teen Challenge.

Bob's link with Teen Challenge was established through bringing a local addict to Christ and then into our programme. Angus had been using drugs for well over ten years when Bob met him and humanly speaking he seemed to be a no-hope case. The regular pattern—in and out of jail—that had developed suggested he would be a user and a loser for the rest of his life, but Jesus had other plans for him. Angus' story is best told in his own words.

'I was born and brought up in Glasgow and I lived and often almost died on the streets there. I could be considered a victim of circumstances since I was only six years old when tragedy struck. My oldest brother stole a beer lorry, lost control of it on a bridge and crashed into the canal. Another brother who was with him managed to get out of the lorry and dived in three times to try to get him out, but he was trapped behind the steering wheel.

'This devastated my parents because they blamed themselves for his death. At the time they were drunk and they never forgave themselves for not stopping my brother's wild behaviour. They began to drink even more, believing it was the only way to drown their guilt and sadness. Less and less control was exercised over me and I began to use their drinking bouts as an opportunity for stealing and getting involved in other illegal activities.

'By the age of 11 I was an experienced thief. The move

to secondary school only made things worse as I met lads from even rougher areas of the city and was soon involved with them. At 13, my friends and I would stay out all night and develop the art of survival. As Glasgow Corporation buses came into the depot for cleaning we'd board them to spend the night under piles of old coats. The cleaners usually hadn't the heart to turn us out; if they did we'd break into partly-furnished houses or bribe a night watchman to let us find shelter.

'It was a crazy way to behave but we needed the sense of identity and comradeship which belonging to a gang provided. We'd all come from families which had been torn apart and could offer us very little hope or purpose, so belonging to the gang seemed to compensate. Before my fourteenth birthday I was sent to an Approved School. I still don't know who approves of it, because I certainly didn't. In fact it just made me aware of things I had never experienced before, including homosexuality.

'I only spent a few months at the school because at 14 I was brought before the High Court in Glasgow on fifty-two charges of theft, burglary, and housebreaking, and sentenced to twelve months' youth custody, which only hardened my attitudes and prepared me for an even worse life of crime. I was convinced that I'd learned all I needed to know—I'd graduated from the Approved School and the Youth Custody Centre with degrees in how to be street-wise and in stealing. My parents had given up hope of controlling me and at 16 I felt I was a "man of the world", convinced that I knew my way around and could survive in any situation.

'It all began to go really wrong when I was 17. People from Glasgow's Drum Chapel area introduced me to the very lucrative business of robbing chemist's shops. There was a ready market for illicit drugs and the profits were enormous, but so were the risks. It wasn't long before I started using the drugs we were stealing—one good haul would last us for three months besides providing all the money we needed. My progress through the various types

of drugs was rapid and within months I found myself
hooked on heroin. My personal hell was to last for seven
years.

'I remember the moment when I realised I was a
junkie: one day on my way to see my mother I suddenly
realised I was addicted to the drugs we were stealing. I felt
desperate and shattered, and I turned round and went
back to the house I had just come from, already withdrawing and needing another injection. Though I knew the
risks involved there was nothing I could do to break free.
Soon a pattern emerged: thieving, arrest, youth custody,
release, then the same all over again. During a four-year
period I was sentenced to thirty-six months in custody, but
even this couldn't break my addiction.

'As our need for drugs increased we began travelling to
the north of Scotland—we were too well known to the
police in Glasgow and had already broken into most of the
chemist's shops there. On one trip alone our haul of drugs
was valued at between £40,000 to £60,000.

'I knew I was fighting a losing battle. For years I had
been injecting drugs but by the time I was 21 I was finding
it more and more difficult. Besides using heroin I had also
injected different types of tablets so the veins in my arms
began to collapse. I looked for new places to inject and
because the veins in my feet collapsed very quickly I used
my neck. I would lie across my bed holding my breath to
make my neck veins stand out and then ask a friend to
inject me. This was dangerous because more often than
not the person injecting was also high on drugs.

'But desperate addicts aren't too careful. Before long
even my neck veins were no good. The only place left was
the groin and I had abscesses where infections developed.
My life was a mess. The constant craving for yet another
fix controlled everything. There seemed no way out and
no power strong enough to make me change—not even
my love for the girl who offered me more than I'd ever
had.

'We'd met when I came out of the Young Offenders

Centre and we fell madly in love. Karen knew I was an addict but I suppose she thought she could change me. She meant more to me than anything else and I really did want to change so that I would be someone worth having. I tried detoxification and rehabilitation programmes, and though I actually completed two I always went straight back to drugs.

'Karen and I loved each other, but even when our first child was born, a beautiful daughter, I couldn't change. Years of addiction had produced in me all the characteristics of a person with a serious life-controlling problem — selfishness, self-centredness and insecurity. I had become an expert manipulator and was emotionally immature and often desperate because of paranoia. How Karen put up with me I don't know; after stealing from her purse I would often disappear for days, but she always took me back. When she became pregnant again she announced it with an ultimatum.

"Angus, I'm going to have another baby, and you must choose between drugs and me and the children. We can't go on like this and you must make your choice!"

'Even as she spoke I knew there was no real choice for me. Much as I wanted Karen I wanted drugs even more.

"Why don't you have an abortion?" I asked. "Get rid of it!" My selfishness and complete lack of principle broke through again, but Karen refused.

"No, Angus" she said, "I'm having the baby and you must decide whether you want us or drugs."

'For me it had to be drugs, but before we could split up God intervened in my life.

'It all began when I "accidentally" met some old friends who had become Christians, and could hardly believe the change in their lives. It was what I needed so desperately but I wasn't convinced it could happen to me. But God wasn't going to give up on me easily. Through my old friends I met Bob Sievwright who became a source of constant irritation. It seemed he had decided to become my shadow — he turned up at the most unexpected times and in the most unusual places. I almost got to the point where I expected him to step out of the fridge when I opened the door!

"Angus, God really can deliver you," he would assure me. "All you need do is give your life to him, let him have a chance. Go to the Teen Challenge rehabilitation centre in Wales—I know that's the answer."

'I wasn't convinced. I'd tried so many programmes and every one had failed. Why should Teen Challenge be any different?

'However Bob refused to give up on me and the situation between Karen and myself seemed more hopeful. I was still using drugs but as long as Bob was there to offer help the circumstances didn't seem so hopeless. At least there was someone who believed I could change. So Karen and I never actually broke up, which was a miracle in itself. When our second child was born, a bouncing baby boy, I knew there would be even more pressure on our relationship.

'Accommodation was a major problem since there were now four of us living in one room, and when the council agreed to rehouse us we were over the moon with delight. I had second thoughts, however, when I discovered who our new next-door neighbours would be— Ann and Bob Sievwright, of course! The net was closing in and about a month after my son was born I gave my heart to the Lord, as Karen had already done some time before. "What you need now," Bob explained to me, "is to be filled with the Holy Spirit. He'll give you the power to live a life free of all your old problems."

'I knew when I gave my life to Christ something had happened but I still couldn't stop using drugs, so maybe what Bob was telling me was the answer. My chance to find out soon came. During a Sunday morning service I went forward to receive the baptism in the Holy Spirit. I fell to the ground under the influence of the Holy Spirit and spoke in a new language.

'I left the meeting knowing that a miracle had happened. For seven years I had been one of Glasgow's best-known heroin addicts, yet as the day wore on I found myself free from the desperate cravings that had become part of my lifestyle. In 1982 I had registered with the Home Office to get supplies of methadone but even that addiction seemed to be broken.

'One day turned into two, then three, and after a week free of drugs I began to believe my transformation was complete. A sense of false security crept into my thinking and by the eighth day I felt strong enough to mix again with my old friends. In no time at all I was up to my neck again in drugs. All my old feelings of guilt and worthlessness came flooding back, as well as disappointment and embarrassment. I knew I'd been foolish and didn't want to meet my new Christian friends, so I deliberately avoided them. I was back to my old habits and tricks but deep in my heart I knew things would never be exactly the same. I secretly longed to get right with the Lord because I knew that what had happened to me was real.

'Although I didn't know it, God was using all these feelings to bring me to a point of total surrender. Before I reached that point I was to know the most heartbreaking moments of my whole twenty-four years.

'My mother announced the bad news. "Your sister Mary's had an awful accident and is in hospital. You'd better get over there quickly because she's in a very bad way."

'Mary was the only member of my family I felt close to. As a single parent with three sons (one actually named after me) she'd struggled to bring them up properly. A breakdown had led to heavy drinking and her children were put into care.

'As we rushed across the city to the hospital my mother filled me in on how Mary's life had gone from bad to worse.

"The remorse of losing the children completely devastated your sister. She gave up on herself and turned to prostitution for money until she went back to the psychiatric hospital for help. A social worker suggested the boys would be better off adopted, and though it was the last thing Mary wanted, she eventually agreed to sign the adoption papers. But she never forgave herself—those boys meant everything to her. Once she realised they would never be hers again she lost her will to live. Today it all came to a head and she decided to end her life. She took some turps and set herself alight and now the doctors are fighting for her life in the Burns Unit."

'I shall never forget entering the room where my sister lay, completely covered in bandages and obviously in a critical condition. I stood by her bed and began to cry as she whispered, "Angus, I've done a terrible thing." I thought she was referring to her suicide attempt, but she added, "I've signed the papers for my boys to be adopted." I felt helpless as I looked at her and without thinking I heard myself saying to her, "Mary, only Jesus can set you free."

'Miraculously, even in my backslidden condition I was able to lead her to the Lord. She only lived a few days longer, but before she died the Lord gave my mother great comfort and assurance. As she was visiting, Mary said, "Mother, there are two men standing at the end of my bed!" My mother, who's not a Christian, turned to look but there was no one there. Shortly after this Mary died. I believe the Lord sent his angels to take Mary to heaven.

'Although Mary's death had a profound influence on me I found myself using even more drugs to block out the pain, remorse and guilt surrounding her death. In it all I knew the Lord was my only answer, just as he had been Mary's, and I sensed that time was running out for me. I had to get right with him but the big question was, "How?"

'It happened almost without warning and in a most unexpected way. No other Christians, no church service, no Bob Sievwright even. Karen had put one of her favourite Don Francisco tapes on and then left me alone in the house. I sat there listening to the lyrics and suddenly felt as if they had been written especially for me.

'Don Francisco was singing,

> I hear your hollow laughter,
>   your sighs and secret pain,
> Pretending and inventing,
>   just to hide your shame.
> Plastic smiles on faces
>   blinking back the tears,
> Empty friends and places
>   all magnify your fears.

'The tears weren't only in the song; they were now streaming down my face and I knew the Lord was speaking to me. I sensed that if I didn't make the right choice I might never get the chance again. God was calling me and I knew that included going into the Teen Challenge programme. On 17 February 1987 I left Glasgow, bound for South Wales and the Teen Challenge centre. I knew by the peace in my heart that I had made the right decision. I had a long way to go, I was aware there were many battles to be fought and many crises to be faced but I knew that with Karen supporting me and the Lord working in my heart, I was going to make it.'

I knew that he would too!

15

By the middle of 1987 the Centre was almost full although we had never advertised our work. The need for larger premises suddenly became very urgent. It had always been my policy to keep the world of 'officialdom' fully informed of all that we were doing but, for better or worse, very little interest had been shown in our work. Whilst we had an excellent relationship with local government, the Welsh Office had always maintained a respectable distance and declined to give any financial help.

It seemed that we fell between two stools as far as grant aid was concerned and there seemed to be no easy solution. The Welsh Office considered it inappropriate to support our Centre with money specifically allocated from central government funds to help Welsh people, when so many residents in our programme came from other parts of the UK. This was certainly the case, but when we approached the Home Office on the grounds that the majority of people we helped were from England, the Home Office quite correctly reminded us that we were under the jurisdiction of the Welsh Office.

In any case, the Welsh Office, whilst recognising the escalating drug problem in the Principality, had not arrived at a policy decision about the need for or support of residential rehabilitation centres. They were concentrating their support on agencies offering information and crisis help as opposed to long-term rehabilitation.

In view of the rather distant relationship we had with the Welsh Office, it came as something of a shock in June 1987 to be officially informed that we were required to register with the County Social Services as specified in the 1984 Registered Homes Act. Furthermore, we were warned that the restricted and limited facilities at our Centre would not meet the minimum requirements of the Act and that new accommodation must be found. The Welsh Office had in effect given us an ultimatum: either find more suitable premises in order to register, or close.

It was a formidable challenge: to register under the Act meant providing accommodation comparable to the standards of an old people's home, plus satisfying the authorities of our competence to operate the programme. The cost involved threatened to be astronomical, even assuming that we found suitable premises. Then history repeated itself, and just as with the White House, another property we had been passing daily to go to our work units appeared to be the answer. About a year previously I remembered one of our students saying, 'That's the building we should have for our Centre, Pastor; it's got so much room. I bet it'll be Teen Challenge's one day!'

'No chance,' I had replied. 'Look at the condition it's in. We've enough on our hands already. I don't think we'll ever be interested in that monstrosity.'

'That monstrosity' was an old supermarket complex of over 14,500 square feet which had been empty for about five years and was in need of a great deal of renovation. Suddenly it became a very interesting prospect—and it was less than half-a-mile from the White House and our work units. It seemed incredible that it had been on the market for five years and that nobody had bought it . . . could the Lord have been keeping it for us? I did not dare tell Gareth or the other staff that I intended to inspect it. It seemed so crazy an idea and humanly speaking it was beyond our ability to repair and our means to finance. But I felt compelled to collect the keys from the estate agent—no harm in looking!

As I entered the old Co-op supermarket my first impression was of the sheer magnitude of it. The fact that it was full of junk and rubbish and that water was dripping through the ceiling did not inhibit my enthusiasm in the least—the place had, like every Teen Challenge student, tremendous potential! Picking my way through what had been the grocery section I walked into the old staff kitchen where overalls and aprons, unfinished packets of chocolate biscuits and other items lay as if waiting for their owners to return.

I walked on and discovered a large deep-freeze section, complete with freezers, bacon slicer and even bottles of sauce and advocaat.

My excitement rose as I crossed into the other half of the ground floor and discovered an area as big as the one I had already seen, and when I climbed the stairs to the first floor I was in little doubt that this was the place the Lord wanted us to have. After completing a quick run around the building I did a slower tour, making a mental note of all the complex had to offer. 'This grocery section would make an excellent dining room and student lounge, partitioned off. The kitchen can easily be converted into a Centre kitchen.' I went into the freezer section. 'This can become two classrooms,' I decided. Moving on to the other side I designated that for administration offices and our own chapel. I was having a great time, lost in my own world but motivated by a power beyond myself—*faith*. The first floor was ideally suited for bedrooms and a games area. 'There,' I thought, 'I've got it all sorted out! I'd better go back and tell the others.'

'Hey,' I almost shouted as I ran into the office, 'I've found our new Centre. It's just the place we need—it's got absolutely fantastic potential. Come and see it!'

Gareth, Ann and Pauline looked at each other and then Ann asked, 'OK, where is it?'

'The old Co-op,' I proudly announced. 'I've got the keys, so come on, let's go and see it.'

I was interested to see what their reactions would be as

we entered through the old double doors. It suddenly dawned on me how depressing the whole thing could look without faith being exercised, so before Ann or Gareth could say a word I confidently announced, 'This area will be the dining room and from here to here will be the student lounge. A corridor will run along here to link up the rooms. Follow me and I'll show you the kitchen, the classrooms and the offices.' I realised how crazy the whole scheme could seem to someone looking at it through purely human eyes, so I tried to be as positive and enthusiastic as possible.

Ann and Gareth followed with hardly a word, except an occasional 'It's so big' and 'It really would make a fantastic Centre', as well as 'But it'll cost the earth to convert it. Look at all the work that needs doing!'

'But if God wants us to have it, it will all get done,' I insisted, though silently I noted the truth of what they were saying.

The central heating system had obviously broken down; cast-iron radiators were cracked through frost damage; the electrical system would probably need rewiring; all the plumbing would have to be renewed; one major wall was bulging in the middle; the roofs needed replacing and extensive dry rot was evident in a large section. Never mind, if this was where God wanted us to be, he would get it all done.

'Well,' I asked as we were making our way back, 'what do you think of it?'

'John, I think it's fantastic,' Gareth said. 'I know there's a lot of work, but I think you should go for it.'

'But it's an enormous project,' Ann warned. 'I agree it could be a marvellous facility, but where are we going to get the money and the labour to do all the work? Don't forget we've got a programme to run. The boys will still need teaching and counselling and that's a full-time job in itself.'

She was right, of course. The task would be formidable but nothing could convince me it was impossible. 'Let's proceed one step at a time,' I suggested. 'First, we need to make an offer and then the problem will be planning permission.' We all knew that this would be the biggest hurdle, apart from finance, especially in view of the problems we had experienced in the early days at Penygroes.

But the application for change of use of the buildings was duly lodged and was granted without any difficulty— a sure sign to us that the Lord was directing the business.

Our next biggest challenge was the finance needed to buy and renovate the run-down buildings. We had already made an offer to buy the complex, subject to planning consent being obtained, and the price had been agreed at £27,500. This was remarkable, not only in view of the extensive accommodation but because it was the same figure as we had offered for the old vicarage. The price seemed reasonable but there was one slight problem—we were about £6,000 overdrawn at the Bank.

'We must launch an appeal at once,' I declared, 'and ask our supporters to find the purchase price. If they're able to do that we can borrow the £35-40,000 needed to renovate it.' We praised God as people began standing with us in faith and sent contributions large and small to help us raise the purchase price, and then at the end of July 1987 our first major donation arrived.

After a long and exhausting day Ann arrived home at about 10.00pm and found a rather crumpled brown envelope lying on our doormat. It had been addressed simply to 'John Macey, Teen Challenge, Penygroes, Dyfed' and posted about a week earlier. It looked insignificant enough, but on opening it she discovered a cheque for £12,000 from someone we had never even met. When I arrived home minutes later Ann met me in the drive, jumping up and down, her tiredness forgotten. 'Look at this,' she cried, 'our first big breakthrough! Praise the Lord!'

I couldn't wait to share this with the students at our chapel service next morning. I felt it was particularly significant that there were twelve in our programme, so as

I told them the good news I added, 'The Lord has prompted this man to give £12,000 and I think we should see it as an investment of £1,000 in each of you. The Lord loves people more than buildings and this is an investment in human lives. Let's praise God for this, but remember also the faithfulness of the old lady in Welwyn Garden City who has sent £5 each month from the first day our Centre opened.'

It was a very moving chapel service as the lads thanked God for touching so many people's hearts. Angus began thanking God for all the kindness being shown and before he could finish his prayer he broke down in heartfelt sobs. Others too were touched by the Lord's graciousness to us.

We marvelled as the money continued to come in and within about two months of launching our appeal we had sufficient funds to complete the purchase. Of course, thousands were still needed to enable the repair and re-modelling work to commence, and once again the Lord's goodness was seen in the way he used so many people to help us. Cheques large and small arrived daily and were a constant source of encouragement to our faith. Executive councils of large denominations as well as small local churches added their support, and each contribution boosted our determination to do what God had shown us.

Grant-making trusts responded to our appeals for help and we were all excited when one of the largest in the UK said they were sending someone to look at our project. I was a little anxious that their representative might feel the task was so enormous and our resources so limited that it would be too risky for the trust to invest in us. I just hoped the visitor would be able to see beyond the mess and share my vision of the finished project. A week or so later she rang me. 'I've just come from my trustees' meeting where we've been considering your project. I thought I'd ring to let you know their decision.' My heart was beating fast: we desperately needed money and obviously their decision had been made. 'We've decided to grant you £25,000,' she calmly announced.

'£25,000?' I repeated sounding rather shocked. 'That's absolutely wonderful, amazing!'

'Well,' she continued, 'my trustees were so impressed with your vision and project that they felt you deserved a flying start. We'll be writing to you soon.'

Cries of 'whoopee' and 'hallelujah' sounded throughout our offices as I announced the news. Ever since then I have tried to answer the phone before anyone else!

16

'Once a junkie, always a junkie!' 'You're nothing but a waste of space and fresh air!' Society has frequently passed these verdicts on drug and alcohol abusers, and the men on our programme were no exception. Gradually they had lost all confidence in themselves and their lack of self-worth and dignity was a constant source of frustration and despair. However our new project—renovating the old Co-op complex—was a God-given opportunity to prove to them and to their critics that the phoenix can still rise from the ashes of disaster and that with God there is always hope.

'Operation Clear-up' was our first priority—getting rid of tons of rubbish, debris and machines left by the previous owners—from safes to slicers, counters to cold-rooms, freezers to fancy fittings. These, with several years' worth of junk, meant lorry-loads of debris to be collected, loaded and eventually carted away to the local dump. Roofs had to be demolished, unsafe walls smashed down, extensive dry rot traced and treated. There were endless opportunities for lads to discover their hidden talents and quite a few became demolition experts.

Amidst the dirt, cold and hard work God was quietly working miracles. The lads learnt to respond to positive leadership. As the staff led by example, sweating and toiling with them, the students realised that teamwork can produce results, that the challenge of adversity can weld men together quicker than most other things. They began to see that the whole project was a modern parable, that God was showing them what he was doing in their own lives—tearing down damaged structures, clearing out the rubbish of sin and laying a new foundation on which he could build.

Daily I was amazed at the feverish activity some lads maintained, whilst even those to whom work had been a four-letter word began to enjoy their assignments. More than once someone called to me, 'Hey, Pastor, I must be going mad or something. Before I came here I wouldn't even work for money; now I'm happy to do it for nothing!'

By January 1988 an enormous amount of work had been done but we seemed only to have gone backwards. Everything we touched seemed to need replacing or reconditioning. On the first floor a whole wall needed demolishing, another was in danger of collapsing, the flat roof had been stripped but not replaced, the metal girders on which the whole building depended showed signs of rusting and needed sand-blasting, and more and more dry rot continued to be discovered. On top of this the electrician's bill soared from an original estimate of £4,500 to around £11,000 and to cap it all, it rained for a solid six weeks! Water pouring through the open roof was blown by storm-force winds into the first floor through the space where a wall was supposed to be and because the sand-blasters had just finished their task the whole place began to resemble the seaside in midwinter.

About 4.30pm one day everyone had gone home early because of the terrible weather. I had stayed behind to assess our progress and the likelihood of our being able to meet the deadline we had set for occupation—July 1988, only six months away. The rain continued to drive into the open building as I picked my way through building blocks, timber and all the usual hazards associated with a building site. I realised why the complex had been empty for so long and why no one else wanted to buy it! They had probably looked at it from a purely human viewpoint and been frightened to death.

'Lord,' I asked, as I stood almost up to my ankles in sand and getting wetter by the minute, 'why did I do it? I must be the biggest fool in Wales.' My heart was sinking; for the first time I wondered whether the project was possible.

'Lord,' I cried out, 'I think we're now in reverse. If you want us in here by July, then please get this operation into overdrive!' Even this prayer—born more out of frustration than faith—was answered, and gradually we saw the project moving forward positively again.

At this time the Lord encouraged us by giving us two new staff members who for many years had been our personal friends. We had first met Robert and Margo Hughes in 1971 when Robert came to Edgware to pastor the church where I was an elder and I worked alongside him until 1976 when Ann and I entered the ministry and moved to Brynmawr, South Wales. The Lord had planned our paths because Robert and Margo moved to Pontypridd, Mid Glamorgan, just before Ann and I moved to Aberdare, twelve miles away. Close links were re-established, especially when Robert and I both became involved with the establishing of Teen Challenge Wales.

Towards the end of 1987 the Lord began speaking specifically to Robert and Margo about joining Teen Challenge. There was no doubting Robert's suitability—for years he had operated a successful counselling ministry whilst his experience in secular employment had equipped him with practical skills invaluable for the occupational training programme. But like Ann and myself three years earlier, accommodation was their biggest problem: they too lived in a church-owned manse. By the end of 1987, however, they had made their decision to join Teen Challenge, trusting God for accommodation—and only six months later they were safely settled in a new house. God had done it again!

As the months ticked by pressure to complete the new

Centre mounted and both staff and students responded gallantly to the challenge. Fifteen-hour days became the norm as staff members volunteered to work evenings and on their only day off each week. David Nicholls, one of our single staff workers, inspired us as he gave himself unstintingly to the task of putting up ceiling boards each night, encouraged by Billy Wylie and sometimes one of the students. God gave extra reserves of strength enabling us to achieve the impossible.

Our task was made all the more demanding because everything had to be done to the highest standards to satisfy the rigid conditions laid down for us by the County Council Planning Officer, senior social workers, architects, electricians, Environmental Health Officer and County Fire Inspector. Each had their own requirements and together they seemed a formidable mountain. No demand was unreasonable, but there were two uncontrollable factors—time was against us and money was running out. By working harder and expanding our work force we could buy a little more time, but for obvious reasons the labour had to be voluntary. The count-down to moving in was on, but so much still needed doing. Artexing, plastering and joinery work remained untouched, and even when these were finished everywhere would still need decorating and thousands of square yards of carpet had to be laid.

Once again the miraculous power of God began working in areas beyond our control. Groups of Christians from local churches responded magnificently to our appeal for workers as Saturday after Saturday their members cheerfully became cleaners, painters and anything else required. Members of the Clydach Full Gospel Church faithfully worked week after week and slowly the outstanding work-pile become smaller.

Needless to say, the project was consuming an enormous amount of money, and because of our lack of financial resources the timescale of work was constantly extended. During the last three months of our run-up to D-Day the Lord again met our financial needs. Unexpectedly we were able to obtain a grant of £27,000 which relieved our finances and allowed us the luxury of hiring extra labour to begin the major task of decoration. Wallpaper and paint alone cost thousands of pounds and we had little problem spending the Lord's money as fast as he provided it.

At the same time our major benefactor, the London-based trust which had generously given £25,000, sent their Appeals Administrator to see how we were progressing. Obviously we made a good impression since we received a further £10,000. These substantial gifts enabled us to press ahead with all the outstanding building and decorating work, as well as laying carpets and purchasing mandatory equipment for the kitchen, that would enable us to move in on target by the end of July 1988. The Lord had worked miracle after miracle for us until at last, like the Israelites, we found ourselves in our promised land!

It all seemed too good to be true. We had been able to transform a derelict supermarket complex into accommodation which was like a comfortable hotel. Shopping areas had been remodelled into lounges, dining rooms, games and teaching facilities, offices, chapels and bedrooms. A major paint company had advised us on colour schemes and the decoration had been carried out to very high standards. Adjusting to the change was quite a challenge—there was a lot more of everything, including cleaning!

We were in our new home but still had to face what had made all our work necessary, the question of registration with the Dyfed County Council Social Services Department. The comings and goings of officials continued with depressing regularity and each visit seemed to result in more to be done and inevitably more financial outlay.

'What do you think's the latest?' Robert Hughes announced after yet another meeting. 'They want us to install an emergency generator—only another £2,000! When's it ever going to end?'

We all realised that before long the final inspection would be held and then we would know—had all our hard work been enough to obtain the coveted Certificate of Registration?

'Lord,' I said as I sped along the M4 towards Swansea on another official errand, 'when are we finally going to be able to get on with the real work—ministering to the lads? And Lord,' I added, 'please encourage us by meeting our financial need; we could do with another £1,000 right now!'

Returning at about 4.30pm that day I was met by a smiling Gareth.

'Have you seen Pauline?' he asked.

'No, I've only just walked in. Why?' I replied.

'Oh,' he said, 'not long ago I took a telephone call from a woman who wanted to speak to you. She said you wrote to her several months ago and she apologised for not having replied to you earlier. However, she said she felt she must phone today to say she'd be sending £1,000!'

'Well, praise the Lord,' I shouted. 'You did hear my prayer and you've answered it already. Hallelujah!'

We approached the day of the final inspection. To our great relief we received a virtually clean bill of health which cleared the way for the Director of Social Services and the county councillors to assess our suitability for registration. Slowly we were getting nearer the day when we could devote all our energies to the purpose for which the Centre had been prepared. The rehabilitation programme had, of course, continued throughout the whole of the renovation work with daily morning and evening studies and as much counselling as was humanly possible. Staff and students had continued to conduct regular weekend services throughout this tiring period since we all felt it was essential to maintain the spiritual emphasis, but by the end of 1988 everyone was feeling the strain of cramming at least two years' work into half that time.

'We've done it!' I announced as I emerged from the

meeting with the Director of Social Services and county councillors.

'Everyone seemed delighted and most impressed with the work we've done. They are also most supportive of our programme and wish us future success,' I assured the staff. 'Our Certificate will arrive in due course but from today we are officially recognised under The Registered Homes Act 1984.'

We could hardly believe it. What had at times seemed impossible had come to pass—months later we realised just how great a financial miracle the Lord had performed so that we could face 1989 with our new Centre completely debt-free. As the accounts were finalised we praised him for his provision of over £180,000 to enable us to complete the building works, despite the fact that the vast majority of Christians in the UK had been unaware of our activities. Once again we had proved that 'in the arithmetic of faith, God is the only figure that counts!'

17

During the last few hectic months of our renovation work Tim entered the programme and immediately became one of our most challenging referrals. Though only 23 his life had been completely wrecked by ten years of drug and alcohol abuse and he knew that unless he received the kind of help that no doctor, psychiatrist or hospital had been able to give him his days were numbered. After nine or ten months in the programme his progress had been remarkable and I well remember the first time he shared his testimony publicly.

'The first 14 years of my life were as normal as any other young lad's. I was brought up in a good home by parents who loved me and made sure I had all I needed. Neither they nor I had any idea how my life would change from that of a stable teenager to a 23-year-old whose only ambition in life was to die.

'I suppose it all started going wrong when I changed schools and got in with the wrong crowd. Until then I'd been doing well and was even told that I had prospects of being a professional footballer. I didn't want to be rebellious or anti-social, in fact I'd always been easy-going, but my new friends introduced me to activities that began to change my whole personality. It started with the odd drink at the weekend, going to the disco and having an occasional sniff of glue during the school lunch-hour.

Within a couple of months I was spending all my money on glue and developed a daily habit. From being a fun-loving, sports enthusiast, I changed into a depressive and aggressive person with frequent violent outbursts.

'At 14 I was a member of a skinhead gang which helped me to get deeper into drinking, glue-sniffing and street violence. By 15 I'd earned a reputation of being a drunken fighter and I enjoyed the status that gave me. In my last two years at school most days were spent glue-sniffing and lying around in a world of semi-consciousness. As I look back I'm amazed that I'm still alive because of the crazy things I did. I remember standing on a railway line one day after getting high on glue. A train was coming and my mates had dared me to stand in front of it to see how near I'd let it come. I was so crazed that my friends had to drag me off the line to stop me being killed.

'Although it was obvious to everyone else that my life was getting messed up I was quite unable to see it myself. By the time I left school all I was interested in was sniffing glue, drinking and having my own brand of "fun". Nights of drinking inevitably landed me in trouble because I'd always go that little bit further than anyone else. I can see now that even my friends were only using me because I was good for a laugh. They'd come round to my house and buy drinks for me so that I'd go out with them and entertain them when I ended up drunk. The trouble was I then became violent so the police were always called. My friends thought it was a good night out—but I was the one who woke up in the morning with black eyes and cuts and bruises all over me. I was the one who had to go to court and pay the biggest fines.

'At 17 my life was going downhill. I began losing weight and drinking even more and got very depressed. My answer was to turn to tranquillisers which I mixed with my drink. My life was a constant round of drinking, fighting, being arrested and then waking up next morning not knowing what I'd done the night before. I began stealing cars which I always left crashed and wrecked. It was a miracle I wasn't killed. At 19 I was admitted to a psychiatric hospital for treatment. I badly needed help to overcome alcohol and drug problems, but after a short period in the hospital I realised it was doing very little to change me. As I mixed with older people who had the same problems I remember thinking, "I'm going to be in this place for the rest of my life!"

'I was one of the youngest there and one day a doctor took me to another ward where there were men whose minds had been burned out through excessive alcohol abuse. I was terrified seeing them run around screaming with wild looks in their eyes. I felt lost but didn't believe the doctor's words: "If you don't stop drinking, either this will happen to you in a few years or else you'll die through liver failure."

'During my stay in the hospital I became friendly with a girl suffering from a schizophrenic condition, and when we were eventually discharged I tried to help her by taking her to my home. It was an unreasonable thing to do because of her unstable state, but when my parents wouldn't allow her to stay I rebelled and this sparked off another cycle of heavy drinking and irrational behaviour. My relationship with my girlfriend ended in a violent outburst in a pub when she hit me and I lost control of myself. I went crazy, smashing people's drinks and fighting in the middle of the road outside. The girl was admitted to another psychiatric hospital and I felt guilty because I felt responsible for putting her there.

'Things went from bad to worse and in no time at all I was living on bottles of cider and was in a virtually constant drunken stupor. Time and time again I woke up in police cells not knowing why I'd been arrested or what I'd done. Even the police began to despair of me.

"You're like a man of 40 or 50," they laughed. "Even your nose is already red! What are you going to do about it?"

'I'd try to act tough but inside I was scared and hurting. I felt inferior and thought there was no way out. I felt trapped by my problem and yet it seemed the only answer. I had to keep drinking because that helped me feel fairly normal but I didn't know when to stop. There was a terribly thin dividing line between drink making me feel normal or turning me into a crazy animal.

'By the time I was 20 the excitement of my lifestyle had long since evaporated and besides destroying myself I was also hurting my family. My mum was having a nervous breakdown because she and my father blamed themselves for my condition. My brothers disowned me because I was a constant embarrassment. I decided there was little point in living and turned increasingly to drugs, so instead of waking up in prison cells I found myself in hospital recovering from attempted overdoses. I despaired of ever being able to break the vicious circle because if it wasn't drink it was drugs; if it wasn't hospital it was a prison cell. I was a problem to everyone and no one knew what to do with me.

'I once spent two weeks in a prison cell—they simply did not have an answer for me. I remember sitting in the cell night after night, alone, scared and confused. I just wanted to die. I couldn't bring myself even to knock on my cell door to ask for a drink of water. Although I was gasping for a drink I went for two days without even a glass of water—I just couldn't face seeing anyone. By the time I was released I'd made up my mind that I'd never get drunk again and I really meant it. I longed to be free to live a normal life, but within two days I'd started all over again. Life became a living hell until eventually I found myself face to face with my doctor.

"If you don't do something I'm going to kill someone and then kill myself," I threatened. Death seemed the only way out. Three other lads I knew had committed suicide: one had taken an overdose, another had set himself alight whilst drunk and the third had walked in front of a train. I began to think my turn was next.

'It was obvious that I must get out of my home town, if only to spare my family more heartbreak, so I made my way to Manchester where I ended up sharing a bench with local tramps. I had hit skid row. Instead of beer and cider it was now surgical spirits and anything I could get my hands on. I'd lost family, friends and self-respect. I had nothing left. I walked around local graveyards, looking at the churches and wondering whether God really existed. I used to sit on the gravestones and think about death and what exactly was put into the grave. Somehow I began to believe that death couldn't be the end and that if I died something inside me would live on—but this only made me more scared than ever. Without wanting to I had entered into a new spiritual awareness which only made life more complicated: I was tired of living but now I was afraid of dying.

'In confusion and desperation I went back to my home town. Inside I was screaming for help. Frequently I cut my arms and throat and one night I lay down on the main road in front of oncoming cars—the only way I knew to cry for help. I moved on again. For weeks I'd been unable to sleep and was troubled by visions of people choking me and setting me on fire. I was convinced that people were out to get me so I bought a gun, determined to kill if necessary.

'New Year's Eve 1988 is a day I'll never forget. I had ended up in Blackpool and the thought of facing another year was too much. I just wanted to die. I walked into a public house and tried to start a fight but I was thrown out onto the pavement. I stood outside without a friend in the world and waves of depression broke over me. All around me was activity and I saw smartly dressed people going off to their New Year celebrations. Dressed in a scruffy old anorak, clutching a plastic bag with all my earthly possessions, I watched the bright lights—and I cried. My world had collapsed.

'I had some money and tried to find a bed for the night, but everyone turned me away because I was so drunk and filthy. Even the local dosshouse was closed. Almost without thinking I made my way to the pier and found myself standing on it thinking how they would find my body in the morning washed up onto the beach. So many times before I had threatened suicide but this was different. I really meant it.

'Then something miraculous happened. God placed his hand on my life, because as I prepared to jump off the pier I heard a voice telling me to telephone my parents. Naturally there was no reason to because I had lost contact with them, but I felt compelled to and so made my way to a phone box. I dialled the number. By now I was completely broken and started screaming down the receiver and banging the windows of the phone box. A crowd gathered and people laughed at my distress which only added to my paranoia. I could hear my father saying, "Come home, son," and myself shouting back, "No, no, no!"

'I wanted to go but I was afraid to. Without thinking, I ran to the station and managed to catch the last train to Wigan. There I made a nuisance of myself in public houses and once again I was arrested.

'New Year's Day 1989 was spent in a police cell—probably the dirtiest one they had. No one knew what to do with me because whilst I was constantly causing aggravation it was not serious enough to send me to jail, and the hospital didn't want me because they could do nothing to cure me. After two days my father was sent for and I shall never forget the pain in his eyes when he saw me.

'Dad sat looking at me and after a long silence said, "Everyone says I shouldn't help you but I'm going to give you one last chance. If you don't grab hold of it then there's nothing I can ever do for you again."

"OK, Dad," I assured him, "I'll never do it again, I promise you. I'll give up drinking."

'A day later I sat shaking in the local Magistrates' Court, terrified that I'd get a prison sentence; under my breath I was praying, "Oh God, please get me out of this one." I didn't really expect God to answer my prayer but a miracle happened right there in court. I was the only person in court that morning to be allowed to go free! Even the police couldn't believe it. The duty sergeant looked unbelievingly at me as he said, "You're the luckiest person alive today to be allowed to walk out of here." He encouraged me to try to sort my life out, get a job and settle down but I wasn't really listening. Even then I could still only think of one thing—to get another drink.

'When Dad took me home I can still remember how shocked I felt when I saw my mother in such a frail, thin and wrecked condition. It was as though she'd grown old overnight and I knew it was my fault. My father echoed my thoughts: "Look what you've done. I'm going to take you away for a couple of weeks to see if we can find a way out of this." I agreed to go but I knew it wasn't the answer. After two days I felt so guilty about everything that I persuaded my father to take me home to try to repair some of the damage.

"Tim, I've got some news for you," my mother said. "I was at church on Sunday and a man was telling us about a place called Teen Challenge—I really believe they could help you." I agreed to meet this stranger and soon I was in David Calland's home listening to what God was doing in so many lives through the work of Teen Challenge. It certainly sounded like what I needed.

'I lived with David Calland and his family while I waited for a vacancy at the Teen Challenge Centre. I was still taking heavy doses of tranquillisers, Valium and any other tablet I could get my hands on. I took them like sweets because they helped overcome my craving for drink. There were times when I felt so desperate that I wanted to leave. One morning I grabbed some money to run out and buy a drink. As I was about to leave the house the telephone rang and someone at Teen Challenge told me there was a place for me. Once again God had intervened in my life with perfect timing and I'm so glad that he didn't allow me to walk out of the house. Soon afterwards I found myself at Teen Challenge.

'It would be a lie to say I found the first few months easy. In fact I recollect very little about them. One thing that does stick in my mind, however, is that though I'd been using such heavy doses of Valium and other tranquillisers I was able to make an immediate break without any withdrawal effects. Although I still had a longing for drink I knew something was happening to me. The worst times were last thing at night and first thing in the morning when I'd reach under my bed out of force of habit to find my drink, and have to face the hard reality that it wasn't there. Many times I felt like leaving but something kept me from doing so.

'My feelings of paranoia were very strong during the first couple of months but even they began to go as the new life of Jesus set me free. Gradually I felt my guilt and shame being washed away as I reflected on what Jesus did for me on the cross. I was a new creation. The Lord had set me free from ten years of drinking, drugging, fighting and smoking and for the first time in all those years I felt free. When I'd been in the programme for four months my parents came to see me and could hardly believe the change. I'm so grateful to the Lord for the way he's helped my family as well as myself, especially the way my mother has recovered her health and the fact that she's become a Christian. I know I have a long way to go but I'm confident that I have a future and I'm really looking forward to it!'

When Tim sat down there were tears in many eyes and undoubtedly everyone had a clearer appreciation of the true meaning of 'the grace of God'. There was no denying that Tim had a long way to go before he could be completely whole in the many areas of his life which had been damaged by horrific experiences, but no one could doubt the incredible changes that had already taken place.

18

As the end of 1989 approached I looked back over the previous five years and with a sense of real gratitude thanked the Lord for all that he had enabled us to achieve. From the early days when we had little more than a burden and a vision the Lord had allowed us to establish amongst drug addicts a work which had become one of the best in the UK. I thought of the dozens of young men who had gone through the programme and rejoiced that because we had been obedient to that vision there were now children who knew a true father's love, wives who had received their husbands free of addictions, parents reunited with lost sons, and many other young men living useful drug-free lives and serving the Lord in various local churches.

Inevitably the thought of those who didn't make it was a sad one, though it was gratifying to realise that of those who completed our programme a very high percentage were leading drug-free lives, and that several who had left prematurely had returned to Teen Challenge for further help.

The Lord had prospered us materially as well. An annual income of £20,000 in 1984 had risen to £256,000 in 1988, enabling our new Centre to be completed. From owning nothing in 1984 the Lord had brought us to the relatively stable condition of having buildings fully paid for and valued at approximately £500,000, although our total income from 1984-1989 had been only approximately £650,000.

By the end of 1989 a five-year cycle had been completed, a new ministry born and established—but I knew our eyes must be lifted to fresh harvest fields.

During the latter months of 1989 new burdens were felt and new direction given by the Lord. I sensed more than ever the need for Teen Challenge to move positively into our nation. Two years earlier in 1987 as I was walking the dog late one night, the Lord had spoken clearly to me about the need to establish a positive strategy of planting new evangelistic outreach centres through a new initiative to be called City Challenge. I sensed the Lord was directing Teen Challenge never to lose sight of its original purpose—to carry the gospel to the streets, to walk where Jesus would walk, to speak to those that he would speak to. Our rehabilitation centre was not to be the goal of our ministry, merely a means to an end, a resource to support street ministries.

As I contemplated this I realised it was a whole new objective, a programme of development which would not happen overnight and which would need enormous resources.

'But where are the workers and the money to come from?' I questioned—not for the first time! 'You know how difficult it is now sometimes to make ends meet. We seem to be running out of new sources of possible finance, so what do we do, Lord?'

'Turn to the Body,' came the Lord's reply. 'Teen Challenge is my work; my Body must be challenged to support it.'

The next eighteen months proved frustrating as far as the City Challenge programme was concerned. The rehabilitation ministry still needed considerable input and at that time the rebuilding programme was also in full swing, but the vision of planting a chain of outreach centres from north to south of the UK continued. It was clear from the stories related to us by lads in our programme that few churches were actively engaged in evangelising troubled young people and that far too often any help available was of the 'hit and miss' variety. So when in early 1989 the chance came to investigate the possibility of opening a City Challenge work in Glasgow I welcomed it as a heaven-sent opportunity.

Frequent referrals from Glasgow to the Centre meant we knew well the needs of young people there so Glasgow had always seemed a 'natural' for Teen Challenge. Furthermore, the fact that the Lord had burdened and guided a local person with a deep concern for Glaswegian addicts was confirmation that he wanted to do something special in the city. Through Bob Sievwright at least half a dozen lads—like Angus—had been referred to the rehabilitation centre and he needed no convincing that Teen Challenge and Glasgow were made for each other.

'What we need is a coffee house where addicts can come for help,' Bob would tell me. 'The whole city is one vast drug problem and though efforts are being made to do something about it, no one has the answer. The message of Teen Challenge is desperately needed in Glasgow.'

Convincing the churches was less easy. Frequent visits to the city convinced me of almost unbelievable apathy amongst ministers. Whilst everyone recognised the need, virtually no one was prepared to get involved. At a meeting with Pentecostal ministers my frustration finally boiled over!

'The drug problem is as bad here as anywhere in the UK and our medical advisor informs me that 86% of intravenous users are HIV positive! That means that in seven to ten years' time you may well be asked to bury a lot of young people in this city. How will you feel if your first contact with that young person is over a coffin?'

I hoped my forthright approach would shame or shock them into action, but only one minister was sufficiently moved to do something. It was agreed that Phil Johnson, minister of the Elim Church in Glasgow, would be chairman of a Teen Challenge Glasgow Committee working with Bob until reinforcements arrived.

Finding coffee-house accommodation at a reasonable price proved impossible. If we could afford it, it was in the wrong place or unsuitable, and if it met our requirements it was too expensive. I threw an alternative at Bob.

'Why don't you consider finding a double-decker bus to convert into a mobile coffee house and counselling centre? In many ways it would be a lot better than a building because you could tour the trouble spots as well as having a much higher profile.'

Bob was enthusiastic: 'I'll see what I can do.'

A few weeks later an excited Bob was on the phone to me.

'John,' he shouted, 'a Christian in the city who owns a bus company has given us a double-decker bus to convert into a coffee house! He's also prepared to service it for two years and to allow us to keep it at his garage—and we can do all the work on his premises. Isn't that wonderful?'

It most certainly was. The next few months saw Bob and a few volunteers working on the bus conversion until in September 1989 it was launched onto the streets of Glasgow by the Lord Provost. Immediately it became so effective that Bob had difficulty coping with invitations to use it, and literally hundreds of young folk were counselled each weekend. Teen Challenge Glasgow was born.

What about Edinburgh, however, generally recognised as having the highest incidence of HIV positive victims outside San Francisco—the city where even official statistics admit that one man in every one hundred between 15 and 45 is HIV positive? Unofficially the figure is feared to be double that and is due chiefly to the huge drug problem in the capital of Scotland. Ought not Teen Challenge to be working on the streets of such a delightful yet desperate city? Thankfully, plans are in hand for such a work in Edinburgh.

Suddenly it seemed that the Holy Spirit had begun

working simultaneously on pastors and churches all over Britain. My phone rang more and more frequently, and often the conversation would be along these lines:

'My church has known considerable growth over the past five years,' the pastor would explain, 'and now we have successful ministries amongst mothers and toddlers, young marrieds and senior citizens as well as our lunch and youth clubs, but God is showing us we have nothing to offer troubled street people and we want to do something about it. Can Teen Challenge help?'

So Teen Challenge continues to grow. Outreach centres are already operating or soon to start in Blackpool, Gloucester, Newport (Gwent), Newcastle-under-Lyme, Glasgow, Swansea and Stoke-on-Trent. The last has been actively involved with street and schools evangelism for the past nine years, and under the leadership of Jim Stinton has been able to gain entrance into five schools to teach the moral education programme.

Invitations continue to be received from churches scattered throughout the UK but one of the most exciting developments has been the resurrecting of the Teen Challenge work in Belfast, which in 1983 had been forced to close through vandalism. Although the existence of drugs in the city is not so obvious as in other similar sized conurbations the uniqueness of its other problems makes it 'custom-built' for Teen Challenge ministries. Life-controlling problems extend far beyond those created by substance abuse and often prejudice, bitterness, bigotry, fear and hatred are more difficult to solve. All these are found in abundance in Belfast where teenagers have grown up against a backdrop of sectarian violence and hypocrisy. In an atmosphere where suspicion, distrust and terrorism thrive, the need for the gospel to be shared on the streets with young people from both sides of the political and religious divide is desperate and urgent.

For many years the Lord had been preparing David Hamilton, a young former para-military terrorist, to lead such an outreach. Whilst serving a ten-year sentence for terrorist activities, David was converted and his life transformed, and in 1989 he joined Teen Challenge's UK work as a very gifted evangelist.

Undoubtedly opportunities in Belfast, indeed in the whole of Northern Ireland, are almost limitless, restricted only by the availability of finance and workers. The alternatives are clear: restrict our activities to what we know we have the resources to achieve, or move ahead in faith with the conviction that God has raised up Teen Challenge in the UK 'for such a time as this'. In my mind there is no question about which we should do!

19

The pieces were beginning to fall into place and an encouraging picture was emerging. Effective street ministries in several cities were already making their mark, teaching seminars were helping to equip local churches to deal positively with people seeking solutions to their life-controlling problems, and our men's rehabilitation programme was proving to be one of the most effective of its kind in the UK.

When our new Centre was officially opened in May 1989, the months since moving in having been used to construct additional bedrooms and vocational training facilities, everyone involved in that aspect of Teen Challenge's work knew beyond any doubt that it was the Lord's blessing on the steps of faith taken just five years earlier. The new complex, which had cost nearly £200,000, had opened free of debt, and was the encouragement we all needed—our spiritual second wind. We had come a long way but we knew there was an enormous journey ahead and many goals to achieve if we were to see Teen Challenge grow into what God wanted it to be.

The need for a girls' programme was becoming an increasing burden in my heart. I had known for some time that we needed to provide for women something similar to the men's programme. It is difficult to describe the feeling of frustration, disappointment and pain I always felt when turning away a cry for help from a young woman. Something had to be done—and as soon as possible! But how?

Where were we going to get a girls' centre? Once again we needed a miracle or it simply would not happen. God was teaching us how to live in situations beyond our control and we were also to learn that what seemed to be permanent solutions were sometimes no more than stepping stones.

In November 1988 a farmer and his wife in Herefordshire quite unexpectedly offered Teen Challenge their farm house to open a new aspect of our work. At that particular time the prospect of further expanding the rehabilitation side of Teen Challenge was something no one was ready to tackle, but by March the following year the challenge was irresistible. A telephone call was all that was needed to find out whether the farmer's offer was still open to us.

'We'd be delighted to see a work for girls at our farm and perhaps in some ways a female centre would be more acceptable than having a lot of men around,' Dick said. 'Now that you've decided to go ahead we'll need to do something about our own accommodation.'

Once again we were in uncharted waters, facing problems which Teen Challenge could not resolve. I wondered at the generosity of Ann and Dick who were prepared to move out of their family house and finance their retirement bungalow in a fantastic gesture of Christian love for troubled young women. Yet I knew another miracle was necessary before they would be allowed to fulfil their plans.

The farm nestled in an idyllic part of South Herefordshire, a picture of tranquillity and a real haven for people from oppressive cities, but it was these very qualities which might eventually make it impossible to use the farm. Planning permission would be needed for a new bungalow on the farm and this was almost unheard of, besides which we would need permission for 'change of use' before the farmhouse could be registered as a Residential Centre. This would mean meeting the local community to secure approval of our plans.

Memories of our nightmare in Penygroes came flooding back and I wondered whether I had enough stamina to face it all for the third time in four years. Even if all these important matters were resolved there would still be the problem of financing the conversion and finding the right staff. Yet again God provided all the resources. In fact, the Lord had been working on the hearts of prospective staff members even before Ann and Dick offered their farm.

In October 1988 when Gareth and I attended a Teen Challenge Conference in Pennsylvania, USA I 'bumped into' a young lady I had last seen some eight years earlier. Sue North had attended a series of seminars which I had led in our coffee house at Aberdare and as a result she had left Swansea to train in Wiesbaden, Germany from where she went to work with Teen Challenge in Austria.

Later, she had moved to Teen Challenge in New York where she had helped to set up and run a girls' ministry in Brooklyn.

'The Lord has dealt with me in a special way, particularly during my time in New York, and I have a great burden to work with young women who need God's healing in their lives. When you start a female ministry in the UK I'd like to be part of it,' she explained.

'Well, we've no plans at present but undoubtedly there's a need for a women's centre, so I'll let you know when it gets started,' I had assured her, though I did not anticipate being able to accept her offer for a very long time.

However, when Sue telephoned me in May 1989 with the news that she felt God was leading her back to England I knew that he was directing her into our future girls' centre.

Sue was not the only young woman that the Lord was working on; when Karen Cooke approached me to share her burden for the girls' centre it was obvious that God was beginning to do something special. Karen and her husband Chris had been involved in work amongst young people for several years and had been responsible for referring a young man from North Devon where they had been living. Through him they had developed an active interest in the work of Teen Challenge, especially the residential rehabilitation ministry, and Karen had often expressed her wish to be involved in a Christian-based programme for troubled young people.

'You know,' she told me one day, 'I can't believe that you intend opening a girls' centre near Hereford! Guess what—Chris has been accepted for a post in Hereford and we'll be moving at the end of 1989. If you think you can use me I'd love to be a part of your staff team,' she beamed.

It seemed too good to be true and yet I knew I should not have been surprised. In his great wisdom and provision the Lord was supplying us with a fully qualified Christian social worker, who with Sue, and Debbie, our third staff member, would make up the initial staff team. In October 1989 Sue and Debbie moved into New Farm to begin the work of setting up the programme and preparing for our first referrals in January 1990. Everything was proceeding smoothly, but in the back of our minds we all knew that some formidable problems had yet to be resolved—in particular, meeting the local community and the planning application for Dick and Ann's retirement bungalow.

'I'd like to welcome Mr Macey from Teen Challenge to our Parish Council Meeting,' the Chairman announced to his colleagues. 'He's written to me about the plans which his organisation have for using Old Farm and I am sure we'd like to hear more about them.'

It was the December meeting of the local Parish Council and I knew the moment of truth had arrived. If previous experiences were anything to go by it could be a difficult examination to pass and I quickly surveyed the faces of both the council members and the dozen or so local folk who had attended. They all seemed friendly enough but I knew only too well that one should not judge an apple by its skin. I was aware that the next few minutes were crucial for the future of Teen Challenge at Ann and Dick's farm.

I need not have feared. Once again the Lord had done his own work and prepared the hearts of everyone concerned. As I sat down the Chairman asked, 'Does anyone have any questions of Mr Macey?'

I looked anxiously at each councillor and could see from their expressions that there was a total lack of any opposition or hostility towards my proposals. After I had answered one or two minor points the issue was put to rest by a Parish Councillor who calmly but firmly remarked, 'If Ann and Dick Jones are behind these proposals there's no need to ask any more questions. They're good people and we trust them.'

As I left the meeting with the other Teen Challenge workers I was thanking God for the way another major hurdle had been cleared, and our confidence and spirits were high.

The day for the South Herefordshire County Council Planning Committee meeting approached. We all knew that a positive miracle was needed to get Dick's application passed. The Planning Officer had visited Old Farm as part of his preparation for presenting the council's case to the Committee, and whilst he assured Dick of the council's sympathetic support for the proposed centre he had clearly outlined their firm objection to the planning application.

'It might be a good idea for you to speak to the Planning Officer yourself,' Dick had suggested to me. 'You could answer any questions about what Teen Challenge intends doing with the farm after I retire.'

My conversation with the Planning Officer was depressing.

'I'm in complete agreement with what you want to do and my Committee feels you are to be commended for the work Teen Challenge is doing. However, we are firmly opposed to granting planning applications for non-agricultural use and there is no way we are prepared to create a precedent by allowing this application. I shall be recommending that the Committee reject the application, but of course, the final decision must rest with the councillors,' the Planning Officer explained to me over the phone.

There was little point in arguing our case. All we could do was pray and ask God for a miracle. And it happened!

Sue was so excited as she discussed the amazing way the application had been dealt with.

'The Planning Committee recommended that the application should be refused, but the councillors disagreed and passed it. What an answer to prayer, eh? Praise the Lord!' she beamed. It truly was, and yet it was no more than we should have expected. God had directed us to the farm and whilst we knew there would be spiritual battles to be fought before his will could be fully implemented, we were confident that in the end he would conquer and give us everything that was necessary to achieve his purpose.

With planning permission secured the way was opening for us to begin accepting girls who needed our help, but one major difficulty still needed to be overcome.

'Dick, the Planning Officer says that until "change of use" has been granted on your farmhouse we'll need to operate on a single household basis, with not more than six people living in the house. That means that with two staff we shall only be able to take two girls and also—here's the big hurdle—you and Ann will have to live with the girls on a family basis. How do you feel about that?' I asked him.

'If it's OK with Ann then I don't mind,' he assured me. 'After all, it will only be until we get our bungalow built, so I'm sure we can manage.'

When Ann heard the news her reaction was the same as her husband's. 'In fact,' she smiled, 'I think I shall enjoy having young people in the house and I'm looking forward to being able to help in any way I can.'

'I think you should be prepared for quite a demanding

148

time,' I cautioned them. 'Living with young people who've come from difficult backgrounds and who have developed life-controlling problems will be a major challenge.'

In January 1990 our first student arrived, escorted from Glasgow by the ever-faithful Bob Sievwright. Mary was 20 and had ended up in a desperate condition through years of drug abuse. Heroin addiction had, as always, taken its toll and when she arrived she knew that the Lord was her only answer. When Beth arrived a little later to join Mary on the girls' programme we were at full capacity.

I often marvelled at Ann and Dick's generosity and willingness to use their home as a Teen Challenge centre, especially as they had no family of their own and were obviously blissfully unaware of the lifestyle and problems of city drug addicts. I sometimes wondered whether the pressure of our programme would prove too much of a strain for them and in April my secret fears were realised. Ann found it difficult to accept Teen Challenge standards on discipline and structure and by the end of April the situation at the farm had reached a crisis point.

'I'm sorry,' Ann said to me, 'but I just can't go along with some of the Teen Challenge rules—I'm sure they're not really necessary and I'd like them relaxed while the programme is in my home.'

It was a situation I had feared but hoped could be avoided.

'I'm sorry too,' I said. 'I'm sorry for any tension or unhappiness that may have been caused to you or Dick. I'm so grateful for all you've done to help our work but I can assure you that, tough as it may seem, young people coming from drug and alcohol backgrounds desperately need the structure which a programme like Teen Challenge gives them.'

I knew by the look in her eyes that Ann could not agree with me and although Dick did not feel as strongly it was obvious and only right that he would support his wife.

'Confrontation is never pleasant,' I continued, 'and even less so when it takes place in your own home. But it's inevitable and a sign that we truly care for these young people.'

I knew, even as I was speaking, that my words were falling on stony ground. There was only one course of action to resolve the situation. Teen Challenge had to move out of the farm.

'Ann and Dick,' I said quietly, 'the last thing I want is for you to be hurt or upset by what's happening. I honestly feel that until your bungalow is built we should move our girls' ministry somewhere else—how do you feel about it?'

'Well,' Ann began, 'we don't want to let you down but I think it would probably be for the best if that happened. But we do want Teen Challenge to come back later in the year,' she added quickly.

I felt confused and disappointed at this turn of events. The Lord had opened a door for us and ensured that one obstacle after another had been overcome, so why had these problems arisen? At the time there seemed no obvious answer but one thing was clear—the girls' work must continue.

The temporary home for Sue and the girls was obvious—the White House. Suddenly I could see why the Lord had led us to it five years earlier and why, despite the fact that we had been trying to sell it for nearly twelve months, no buyer had appeared. Once again I was learning to trust God's plans and when the girls moved into the house it all began to feel so right.

At this time we were still looking forward to returning to Herefordshire and when in June 1990 the necessary permission for 'change of use' was granted by the Planning Department of South Herefordshire District Council it seemed another confirmation of the Lord's guidance. Funds began coming in for the extensions and renovations and in good faith plans were drawn up and submitted for approval. But despite all the outward signs of success and progress I knew that under the surface everything was not right and that it was beginning to look more and more likely that we would never return to Herefordshire.

In November on one of my regular visits to the farm Ann said, 'I must be honest with you: I can't find any peace in my heart about proceeding with our original plans. I'm sorry about how I feel, but we can't do anything more until I find the peace I need.'

In reality it was the end of the road for Teen Challenge at the farm. Again I felt disappointed and confused.

'Why, Lord, has all this happened?' I questioned. 'Why all the progress, the miracles and now a dead end?' I was searching for answers. Ann and Dick had even built their bungalow and the whole situation was an embarrassment to them, as well as a genuine disappointment. Surely there must be some explanation, some reason? And then it came.

'It doesn't matter where the ministry is located,' the Lord said. 'The important thing is that it was started. Without the Hereford situation you would never have moved forward in faith. I can close doors as well as open them and now you must establish yourselves in the White House. You saw me perform a miracle to give it to you and you will see many more miracles in the lives of those I bring to it.'

So that was it! The White House would be our new girls' centre, just five hundred yards from the male centre and perfectly equipped for such a purpose. The Herefordshire experience had not been wasted; it was the catalyst that had helped to bring about the new ministry. In order to accommodate a reasonable number we would still need to obtain registration, extend and again remodel the house, all of which would cost virtually the same as the project at the farm. We had weathered some stormy experiences which had only served to strengthen our resolve to see through what God had begun.

The close proximity of the girls' centre meant that my involvement with it inevitably increased and I was amazed to discover the difference in atmosphere between the male and female programmes. The girls' centre, of course, was much smaller than the boys' accommodation and this created a distinct sense of homeliness and domesticity. It was exciting to see God healing emotions damaged or even destroyed by many disastrous relationships.

The legal restriction on the number of girls in the programme at any one time also ensured that they were able to receive virtually one-to-one attention, and as Mary and the others began building meaningful relationships with their counsellors it was amazing to watch their spiritual progress. By the end of 1990 Mary was preparing to leave the Centre, excited at the prospect of graduating and for the first time in her life enjoying real success.

The big night arrived on 1 February 1991 when a crowded church celebrated with her the joy of a life radically transformed. A despised heroin addict had been changed into a radiant and beautiful young woman. Over the years we had seen dozens of young men complete the programme and whilst every graduation service is special, there was something unique about seeing our first girl graduating from the Teen Challenge programme. There were many moist eyes as Mary shared her testimony, convincing everyone present that the disappointments and even heartbreaks were all worthwhile.

'Glasgow is full of broken homes and I came from one, only mine was broken by my father's death. I can't remember it because I was just two and my clearest memories only start from the time I was eight. I wish I could blank out everything that happened until a year ago because most of my childhood and teenage years are a nightmare to remember. Though I know that's impossible, I thank God that he's healing me of the emotional damage those years inflicted. Coming to know Jesus is the most wonderful thing that has happened in my life.

'After my dad died my mother married again and that was the beginning of my problems. My step-dad never accepted my two brothers and me as part of his family and after my mother had three more daughters our family was split into two; it was them and us as far as my step-dad was concerned. We were denied any privileges or love, and although my mother was terribly hurt by his behaviour there was very little she could do, especially when he began drinking heavily.

'Now that I'm a Christian I can see that everyone is responsible for their actions but I can't help thinking that many of my attitudes were formed by the behaviour of my step-father, which I could do absolutely nothing to control or change. As his drinking got worse so did his violence and I can remember my mother, my brothers and myself huddled together waiting for him to come home at night. We were petrified when he was drunk because we knew he would beat up my mother, so our young lives were constantly overshadowed by fear, rejection and even a sense of anger and revenge. I can remember many occasions when my eldest brother fetched the police to save my mother from being badly hurt, and although my step-father was taken into custody for the night he was released next morning and we knew it would soon happen all over again.

'This went on until I was 10, and then I could hardly believe our luck. My step-dad left home. It seemed too good to be true at first and we would all sit up at night with my mother waiting to hear his footsteps coming down the path. Every taxi that drove up the street made my heart miss a beat because I thought it was bringing him home. I needn't have worried because he never returned. In a strange way though, my step-father's absence from home was a major reason for the trouble I got into. My mother began spending more time with her friends and I found myself with more freedom than I'd ever known.

'My step-dad used to keep us kids indoors as soon as we came home from school, to make life as miserable as he could for us. But with his departure I began spending more time with friends and in no time I was smoking and sniffing glue. I was only 11 and didn't realise I was becoming addicted to glue. I was also drinking.

"I got rid of one problem in the family when your father left," my mother would say, "and now you're starting." It wasn't unusual for the police to bring me home after they'd found me glue-sniffing. My brothers often gave me good hidings to try and make me change, but the more people tried to stop me the more determined I was to continue. When my glue-sniffing was at its height I became friendly with a girl at school who encouraged me to give it up. She invited me to her house where I discovered she was smoking pot. Although I preferred the effects of glue I was influenced by her and I began to share in her drug habit and in the activities of other young people that she hung around with.

'Life then became much more sinister as I was introduced to the world of hard drugs. I was still only in my early teens, the lifestyle of these heroin addicts really did seem attractive, and besides I had a tremendous respect for my friend. We were so close we were like sisters. I didn't use heroin immediately but was introduced to dihydrocodeine tablets. Within months, however, I was mainlining on heroin. It seems crazy now but at the time all this was going on I was genuinely enjoying my lifestyle—even all the wretched things I had to do to get money for my drugs.. I had quickly developed all the survival techniques of a drug addict and I didn't care about anyone except myself. There were times when I should have gone to prison for the offences I'd committed to get drugs and it was only my age that kept me from getting a custodial sentence.

'By my mid-teens my life was really messed up, and although I refused to acknowledge it, I was also bringing disaster and grief into the lives of my family as well. Despite everything I did my mother always stood by me. I stole, lied and cheated her but she always refused to kick me out. My sisters got so fed up with me that they left home, my brothers refused to have anything to do with me and then, worst of all, my mother had a nervous breakdown. That really got to me because I knew it was my fault. I loved my mother more than I'd ever admit and it tore me in two to see the pain I was causing her. I just knew that I must do something to change before it was too late.

'Everyone's heard the expression "once a junkie, always a junkie" and I began to believe it was true of me. I knew I couldn't do it by myself so I decided to try some rehabilitation centres. Over the next two years I went to four different centres but as soon as I left them I was back to my old tricks, returning to the only lifestyle I knew— the drug culture, the street people and the sense of security they gave. By the time I was 21 I felt that my life was a disaster. I was at the end of the road and there really was nothing worth living for.

'Whilst I was in this state of total hopelessness someone told me about Jesus. I had been brought up in the religious atmosphere of Roman Catholicism and I didn't know it was possible to have a personal relationship with Christ founded on real love. I was amazed when I went to church for the first time and heard that God wanted to help people, even while they were deep in their problems. I knew God was speaking to me but I wasn't sure he could help me. After all, I'd had years of listening to people telling me I was a waste of time, a waste of fresh air and a waste of space, so why should everything suddenly be different?

'For four months I stayed with various Christians from the church and they really showed me true love and support, but I knew I hadn't changed and there was nothing they could do to make it happen. I was reaching a point where I felt that the church was no better than the rehabilitation centres I had been in—it wasn't proving to me that I could confidently face the future without a drug dependency problem. I felt there was only one thing I could do—go back to where I belonged, back to the drugs, drink and crime.

'But God had spoken to me; he really wanted me and just as I was about to turn my back on him I heard about Teen Challenge. Before I knew it I was out of Glasgow into the girls' programme. God had stepped into my circumstances and at last things were about to change dramatically.

'I hadn't been in the Teen Challenge programme very long before I realised that if I wanted to find God's answers to my problems I had to let him have his way in my life. I began to let Jesus have full control over me. Christ revealed himself to me and showed me that he is real. I'm finding that my insecurity is being turned into security in him. His love is overwhelming and I can confidently say that drugs are no longer an issue for me because Christ has set me free.

'Teen Challenge was the chance I needed. It hasn't been easy to stay in the programme and face my problems and the truth about myself, but for the first time in my life I've completed what I began. I look forward to my future with confidence because I know that Jesus will be with me.'

God had been gracious to Mary and, through her, to us as well. As she had said, she had completed what she had begun and a new young woman was about to embark on the next stage of her great adventure in God. She was moving on, leaving behind the hang-ups, fears and inhibitions which had dogged her young life for years. For Mary there was hope and a future but we all knew that there were probably hundreds more like her huddled somewhere on the streets of our cities. Mary was living proof that miracles happen, all the encouragement we needed to redouble our efforts to guarantee that no one, fellow or girl, would be denied the chance to prove that Jesus is the life-changer and the real joy-giver.

Teen Challenge in the United Kingdom was doing what God and David Wilkerson had always intended, helping where people were hurting, proving that God is still in the caring business, that junkies, addicts, homosexuals, criminals and alcoholics don't have to stay that way. Teen Challenge had become a testimony to a confused and crushed world that God is for real!

I realised as I looked at Mary that, like it or not, I had become enmeshed in something that was more than a ministry; for me Teen Challenge is a lifestyle—even, some might say, a life-controlling problem!

Postscript

The years which have passed since our rehabilitation centre was opened have helped to give a clearer picture of the effectiveness of the programme. People, unlike commodities, cannot be treated as statistics or shown as graphs of targets achieved. Everyone who has entered Teen Challenge has been unique and it is therefore quite natural that great interest is shown in the progress of graduates. The stories contained in the earlier chapters have been about real people with real problems who need real answers! Thankfully the majority have left Teen Challenge to prove that Christ is a real Saviour who offers permanent help for all of life's trials and challenges. Sadly, there have been the disappointments as well, but they are definitely in the minority.

Tim, our converted Hell's Angel and early staff member at Teen Challenge, emigrated to the USA after marrying an American. His close friend Paul has had a hard struggle since leaving and has suffered several set-backs. Amazingly he still shows great interest in spiritual things but he experiences difficulty in finding Christians to whom he can relate effectively.

One of the greatest joys of working in Teen Challenge is to see former students serving the Lord, sometimes in full-time Christian work. Two of our graduates are currently working with Teen Challenge after a couple of years in secular employment. Peter, the football hooligan and alcoholic from Birmingham, married a local Welsh girl and they now have a delightful son. Peter is leading the Teen Challenge evangelistic work in Swansea and also runs an effective schools programme. His exciting presentation of God's deliverance in his life continues to open many doors and he is often able to share his testimony in churches around the country. Angus is now a staff member at our Centre after having completed a training course in bricklaying on leaving the programme. He then had a successful period as a self-employed builder but he could never suppress the call of God to serve others who needed the same help that he had received.

Little Jim and Brian continue to do well. Jim is living in the Midlands where he has held the same job for several years. Brian, after a shaky start, has established himself in a financial consultancy business and is married with two beautiful children. Both are actively involved in local churches.

One of our saddest disappointments is still painful to write about. Big Jim was a man I had come to love and respect and after sharing many services with him I knew God had a special purpose for his life. It is still a mystery how he allowed himself to be drawn back into the drug world, even though he had been badly let down by someone he had greatly respected. Despite numerous attempts to help him Jim became more and more difficult to get through to, chiefly because he felt he had let so many people down. His drug problem escalated and ended tragically in June 1991 when he died of an overdose of heroin. His funeral was the saddest I have been involved in, but also served as a vivid reminder of the life and death nature of the work which God has called Teen Challenge to do. Sadly Jane also became involved in the drug scene after his death, and one of their two boys has been taken into care.

Colin is now happily married and is a partner in his father-in-law's successful carpet business. His change of lifestyle has something of a 'fairy story' ring to it and Colin is now the Youth Leader at the Swansea Elim Church.

Tim's story since leaving Teen Challenge also emphasises the difficult nature of rehabilitation work. Patience, understanding and tough love are essential ingredients for anyone who feels called to help people with life-controlling problems! Tim entered a Bible School on leaving Teen Challenge but shortly after graduating began to slip back into some of his old behaviour patterns. I do not doubt that he still has a sincere desire to follow the Lord but he is struggling to find answers to deep problems in his life.

The young people whose stories are contained in this book are representative of the thousands more in our country who need help. The odds against Teen Challenge are enormous but as the drug problem continues to escalate there can be no doubt that this faith ministry must go on.

Teen Challenge UK

Teen Challenge is active in the UK in the following areas of work:

Evangelism

Evangelism is the reason for the existence of Teen Challenge, and various centres operate in the UK to reach troubled people. These are often linked with coffee houses and active local churches.

Details of this and ways in which Teen Challenge can help local churches in evangelism are available from the National Office.

Rehabilitation

Separate residential Christian discipleship programmes are available to men and women (generally in the age range 18-35 years) who wish to recover from drug and/or alcohol addictions. Information on these programmes and the referral procedure is available from the National Office.

Seminars for Training and Equipping Local Churches

Teen Challenge is able to offer local churches two major seminars which can form the basis for sound church growth.

1. *Lifestyle Power Evangalism*
   'Invaders of the Lost Cities'—a seminar to mobilise God's army to win our nation for Jesus Christ.

2. *Turning Point*
   A dynamic seminar designed to equip local churches with a programme to help people live by biblical principles. It is especially relevant to those with life-controlling problems and to others who wish to avoid them.

Further information on these seminars is available from the National Office:

> Teen Challenge UK
> Penygroes Road
> Gorslas
> Llanelli
> Dyfed
> SA14 7LA
> South Wales
> (Tel. 01269-842718)

National School of Evangalism

A bi-annual three-month School of Evangelism is held to train local church workers and volunteers for Teen Challenge ministries. The school offers two months of residential teaching and a further one month of practical experience at a Teen Challenge centre. Full details can be obtained from:

> Jim Stinton, Training Director
> National School of Evangalism
> Stoke Road
> Shelton
> Stoke-on-Trent
> Staffordshire
> ST1 4DQ
> England